Perspectives on Contemporary Theatre

Perspectives on Contemporary Theatre

OSCAR G. BROCKETT

Louisiana State University Press / Baton Rouge

ISBN 0–8071–0939
Library of Congress Catalog Card Number 75–154268
Copyright © 1971 by Louisiana State University Press
All rights reserved
Manufactured in the United States of America
Printed by the TJM Corporation, Baton Rouge, Louisiana
Designed by J. Barney McKee

PREFACE

The essays which follow have been shaped by the occasion for which they were originally written. Each summer since 1935 the Department of Speech at Louisiana State University has held a conference at which a speaker has delivered a series of lectures. In 1970 I was privileged to participate. This book is the result.

These essays are designed for a general rather than a specialized audience. Those who attend the conference represent all areas of speech, some of which are only peripherally concerned with theatre. Consequently, in writing the essays, I assumed that this audience would be interested in my overall topic but would have little detailed knowledge of it. Thus, while I hope they will concur in what I say here, specialists in contemporary theatre will probably find little new in it. On the other hand, I trust that the general and nonspecialized reader will encounter much that is both new and enlightening.

My goals were to increase understanding of today's theatre by exploring current practices and issues, and to provide perspective on them by pointing out some forces and ideas that have gone into their making. Therefore, the essays deal as much with the background as with contemporary practices themselves. It was not my purpose either to advocate or to denounce recent developments. I wished merely to generate understanding, so that my audience might approach today's theatre knowledgeably, for worthwhile judgments depend upon informed opinion rather than prejudice and impression. Thus, I have tried to explain both where we are and how we have gotten there.

The number and length of the essays were determined by the six occasions on which I spoke and the fifty-minute time periods into which my remarks had to be fitted. Obviously, other topics might have been treated and those that were discussed might have been developed at greater length. But I chose those that seemed most crucial and discussed them as time permitted.

Since these essays are tied so closely to an occasion, I have revised them little. It seems to me that my audience at the conference was representative of a much larger public and that many readers can come to these essays in print as that audience came to them as lectures—with interest but without specialized knowledge. It is for them that the book is intended. I have altered slightly the beginnings and endings of some essays (those originally tied too specifically to the occasion), I have sought to sharpen some points, and I have added some notes. But for the most part, the lectures are published as delivered. I shall be gratified if my readers receive them with the same interest as did my listeners.

I would like to express my sincere appreciation to the faculty of the Department of Speech, both for inviting me to give these lectures and for many courtesies during my visit. I am especially grateful to Professors Waldo Braden, Claude Shaver, and, above all, Gresdna Doty, whose thoughtful arrangements permitted all to go smoothly.

CONTENTS

Perspectives on Contemporary Theatre

ONE / The Contemporary Theatre: An Overview

Today the theatre is often a source of controversy almost as great as that surrounding the society which it reflects. For example, it is now difficult to watch television without hearing some reference to nudity in the theatre. On late-evening "talk shows" the favorite question to actors seems to be, "Would you appear nude on the stage?" for nudity seems to have crystallized in the public mind a whole range of issues about the contemporary theatre. But the introduction of nudity is only the most obvious innovation among many which since World War II have altered the theatre drastically from the institution fondly remembered by those who deplore the changes. The conservative theatregoer must now search more diligently than in the past to find entertainment that will permit him merely to relax and enjoy himself or to discover a thoughtful play that does not require him to acquiesce in the mockery of much in which he believes.

But, if the conservative theatregoer deplores the changes, his radical counterpart usually finds them disappointing, for he considers the typical Broadway fare an insult to his intelligence in its obvious appeal to the affluent. Even the more experimental productions often seem to him insufficiently committed to change, for he wishes to see the theatre used as a weapon for reshaping society.

Probably the majority of playgoers falls somewhere between these two polar attitudes. Nevertheless, the poles serve to clarify the conflict in which the contemporary theatre is caught, just as they mirror the conflict in which our society is caught. As is society, the theatre is faced with conflicting demands: on the one hand, that it resist change; and on the other, that it restructure itself completely.

That the theatre should become an object of contro-versy was almost inevitable, for, since it always reflects the values of the society it serves, it would have to remain truly insulated from life if it were not to become caught up in the issues of its time. In fact, of all the arts, the theatre, because of its very nature, is most apt to become a battleground for changing values—a point that can be better understood by looking briefly at the theatre in relation to the other performing arts, especially music and dance. Although these arts are alike in requiring performers and an audience, they are significantly differ-ent in the kind of relationship they establish between performer and audience. It is the special nature of this relationship which makes the theatre so vulnerable to controversy and criticism.

In music, rock and folk (or pseudofolk) have attracted most attention in recent years. Often the songs embody protest or seem to encourage attitudes and behavior— usually relating to sex, drugs, or politics—considered by many to be reprehensible. But each song can only distill one emotion or explore a limited range of attitudes or ideas. It projects a concentrated state of feeling rather than being the enactment of an event; it emphasizes a response rather than the act itself.

Dance, like theatre, is a three-dimensional medium in which the live performer is in direct visual contact with the spectator. Because it communicates primarily through stylized movement, however, it tends to be distanced from the audience. Seldom are acts performed in a realistic manner. Consequently, the audience is given the essence of deeds, situations, or emotions. And, although nowadays dance occasionally employs words, normally it is a nonverbal medium and therefore limited in its conceptual range.

If television and film are included among the performing arts, the distinctions become more complex, for the theatre then is only one among other dramatic media. Nevertheless, the audience-performer relationship in the theatre is quite unlike that in television or film.

In many respects, television is the most immediate of all media. With it, real events may be seen as they are actually occurring. But it differs significantly from the theatre in at least two ways. First, it is two-dimensional. It converts everything into pictures, which tend to obscure the distinctions between fictional and factual programs. For example, it has been argued that the war in Vietnam is difficult to comprehend because it flashes across television screens so often and so like the dramas between which it is sandwiched. In the news reports, human beings are actually killed but their deaths make little more impression than do the fictional ones seen in dramatic programs. Sometimes the actual deaths make even less of an impression because viewers normally come to know the fictional victims and so feel for them more deeply than they do for real human beings of whom they have never heard and about whom they know nothing—except that the victims are human and that it is sad for any human to suffer and die. Consequently, it is an ironic fact that on television real events often seem less concrete and less touching than do fictional ones.

Second, in America most television is dominated by advertisers. Except on educational stations, programming is controlled by sponsors who are concerned with attracting the largest possible number of potential buyers of their products. Consequently, most sponsors seek to avoid controversy. Although each year the frontiers of acceptability are altered somewhat, television remains an essentially conservative medium because of its determination not to offend potential customers.

Television now has much of the appeal formerly exerted by films. Before World War II, it was the movies that captured the mass audience with works designed to attract the greatest possible number of spectators. Like television, film was then for the most part conservative. After the war, however, as television captured an increasingly large share of the potential audience, filmmakers had to reassess their role. Thus, they became more adventurous both in subject matter and treatment than either television or the theatre of the 1950s. Many of the things that now outrage theatre audiences were being done in films long before they found their way onto the stage. Furthermore, the movies remain more adventurous than either theatre or television.

Nevertheless, the theatre is more subject to controversy than is film because of one significant factor—the relationship between performer and spectator—for there is a basic difference in the psychological response aroused by watching pictures of an act and in watching the human actor in all his three-dimensionality performing the same act in what amounts to the same room with the audience. In the live theatre, the psychological distance between spectator and performer is greatly reduced from that created by film. Thus, although many more persons in the United States have seen *I Am Curious (Yellow)* than have seen *Oh! Calcutta!* the latter seems to have made a greater impact on public consciousness and to have become a symbol of the moral laxity of our society.

The differences in the psychological relationship between spectator and performer in a film and in the theatre can be illuminated by considering attitudes toward private as opposed to public acts. For example, there are a great number of subjects that most persons are willing to discuss frankly with friends in private that they would dislike being questioned about in the presence of others, many of whom may be total strangers. This distinction can be illustrated further by considering briefly responses to the off-color joke. Some persons would probably be outraged by such an anecdote under any circumstances. Many, however, are probably willing to listen to, and enjoy, such jokes among close friends and in privacy. But as the group enlarges and the privacy vanishes, fewer are willing to countenance them. The joke itself may not have changed, but the psychological relationship to it is altered by the circumstances. This variation in response can be likened to the audience-performer relationship in the performing arts, each of which differs from the others in explicitness and publicness.

The theatre is at once the most explicit and the most public of the arts. It is the most explicit because in drama live actors representing human beings are shown performing deeds like those of real life. It is the most public because the audience is exposed to the deed itself, rather than a picture of the deed (as in the movies) or an electronic transmission of the deed (as in television) or a highly stylized distillation through movement (as in dance) or a lyrical or emotional version of the deed (as in popular music). The publicness and explicitness of the theatre, therefore, make it subject to controversy more intense than that to which the other performing arts are subjected.

Because of its three-dimensionality and its publicness, the theatre has also become attractive to those who are seeking an artistic medium that can be used as a weapon in the struggle over political and social issues. Although both television and film have a wide range of means available to them and may present problems more graphically than can the theatre, they cannot match the psychological relationship between performer and actor created by the live theatrical situation. A confrontation may be shown on television or film, but a direct confrontation between the doers and the watchers cannot be achieved in those media. At times, everyone probably does talk back to his television set, but obviously those on the screen do not hear. The theatre, on the other hand, can and has been used to force confrontation between spectator and actor, one more often precipitated by performers than audience, it might be added, but confrontation nevertheless. In the theatre, the actor can come down into the auditorium and the spectator can go up onto the stage, and those who have recognized the potential of theatre as a weapon in controversy have utilized these possibilities to advantage. Perhaps even more to the point, the live performer does not have to remain in a theatre building at all; he may go out into the streets and seek out an audience that would not voluntarily attend a theatre, or he may engage in "guerrilla theatre" by interrupting meetings or public ceremonies with unscheduled performances of skits which dramatize issues.

It is probably these attributes of the theatre which have attracted many new practitioners to a form long considered ailing, even dying. Many of those who make up the new breed of theatrical workers probably would have shunned the theatre twenty years ago as hopelessly outmoded (although it must be admitted that many still do). While the recent upsurge of interest does not herald any drastic change in the theatre's fortunes, it is an encouraging change, for the theatre's popularity has been declining for almost a century. Perhaps some perspective on the present can be gained by looking briefly at that decline.

During the nineteenth century the theatre reached the peak of its popularity, for industrialization led to an enormous increase in the urban population and consequently in potential audiences. Furthermore, until near the end of the century the theatre had no strong competitors seeking to wean away its patrons. Thus, it was able to satisfy a wide range of tastes by presenting an extremely varied repertory which included on each bill not only a full-length play but a short farce or musical piece, singing and dancing, and variety acts of all sorts—comedians, trained animals, acrobats, and novelties now more usually associated with carnival side shows.

Although the potential audience has steadily increased throughout the past century, the competition for patrons has also intensified, and the theatre has waged a losing battle as new attractions have continued to appear. Among the theatre's most effective competitors have been spectator sports. Obviously sports of various sorts have existed throughout history, but the commercial exploitation of them has been underway only since the late nineteenth century.[1] For example, the first professional base-

[1] A good survey can be found in Walter Umminger, *Supermen, Heroes, and Gods: The Story of Sport Through the Ages,* translated and adapted by James Clark (New York, 1963). There are several histories of individual sports, among them Allison Danzig and Joe Reichler, *The History of Baseball* (Englewood Cliffs, N.J., 1959), and Allison Danzig, *The History of American Football* (Englewood Cliffs, N.J., 1956).

ball team was formed in 1869; then in 1876 the National League was formed and in 1900 the American League. The popularity of this sport was such that it soon came to be called America's national game. The first professional football game was played in 1895 and the sport has steadily grown in popularity since. Spectator sports also include basketball, racing, boxing, wrestling, and a host of others. Among them they have come to attract a far larger audience than dramatic performances can command and have siphoned off many of the theatre's former patrons because they exert many of the same appeals as does drama—opponent pitted against opponent, conflict and resolution, the exhibition of skill in excess of that possessed by the spectator. Perhaps equally or more important, sports carry with them the aura of manliness and so they have become acceptable to many who consider the theatre effeminate. Consequently, in the twentieth century, the number of women who attend the theatre far exceeds the number of men.

Even those who remained faithful to dramatic entertainment came to be faced with choices between the theatre and other media offering programs at lesser cost. The first of these was the silent movie. Motion pictures were inspired by goals also felt in the theatre: to render reality as faithfully as possible. Consequently, they gradually evolved from the desire to capture lifelike visual images, for painting, no matter how realistic it became, still seemed to many persons artificial. The first result was photography, which developed in the first half of the nineteenth century out of Louis Daguerre's experiments. But a photograph, like a painting, can only capture and fix visual appearance at a single instant. The problem then became how to make one picture fade into another and so seem to move. The major breakthrough came in the 1890s, when Thomas A. Edison demonstrated his kinetoscope. But, although it captured motion, the kinetoscope could only be viewed by one person at a time. It remained for George Eastman to invent a flexible film and for Thomas Armat to perfect a projector. Together these inventions made it possible to create crude silent entertainments. To house them, nickelodeons were opened beginning around 1905. Novelty and low admission costs made the new medium such a success that within four years there were 8,000 movie houses in the United States. Despite this large number, they did not at first make a serious dent in attendance at plays, for the early motion picture theatres normally seated only about 100 persons. But in 1914, the opening in New York of the Strand Theatre with its 3,300 seats began the trend toward large houses.

At approximately the same time, significant changes were being made in films themselves. Up to about 1915, movies were short and programs were made up of several works. Then, D. W. Griffiths and others began to make full-length films which provided the same powerful emotional appeals as did melodrama and presented spectacle far beyond what the theatre could offer. Consequently, after World War I, increasing numbers of spectators deserted the theatre for the movies. This trend was accelerated in the late 1920s as a result of two new elements: in

1927 sound was added to the previously silent film and thus one of the theatre's principal claims to superiority vanished; and in 1929 a serious economic depression began. Since audiences could go to the movies for a fraction of what it cost to see a play, theatregoing became a luxury which few could afford, especially as the depression deepened. Until the 1930s, the theatre had not really felt the pinch of competition, for despite the exploitation of spectator sports and of movies, the potential audience had grown at such a pace that actual attendance at the theatre had increased, even though the percentage of the total audience had steadily declined. But after 1930 the theatre began noticeably to lose ground. Increasingly it had to woo the relatively affluent middle class, and it came to be, even more than in the past, a form catering to a minority audience. By the end of World War II, the American theatre had been reduced to about thirty theatres in New York City and a small number of touring companies originating there.[2]

Following World War II, both theatre and movies were dealt a severe blow by the introduction of television. The kind of entertainment that films had offered at low prices was now provided free by the new medium. This development came at a time when the price controls that had been in effect during the war were removed and when production costs both in the theatre and in film-

[2] For detailed treatments of the film, see Richard Griffith, *The Movies: The Sixty-Year Story of the World of Hollywood and Its Effect on America from Pre-Nickelodeon Days to the Present* (New York, 1957) ; and Arthur Knight, *The Liveliest Art: A Panoramic History of the Movies* (New York, 1957) .

making soared. Furthermore, television had an additional advantage—the audience did not have to leave home to see it. Now the film as well as the theatre had to base its appeals on special grounds. One of these was familiar: vehicles with stars sufficiently attractive to make people willing to undergo the inconvenience of getting to the theatre. It was the appeal of the "night out," of the special occasion, of seeing the latest hit, of diversion from the daily routine. On Broadway it became almost a necessity for the producer, if he was to recover his investment, to have a show capable of attracting spectators in large numbers despite the high prices. This, in turn, meant making a calculated appeal to the mass audience, and consequently most producers avoided controversial subjects and techniques or adopted them only with caution. This situation has remained typical of Broadway, for, although it takes in new subject matter and new techniques, it does so usually only after they have proved commercially viable.

The calculated appeals made by Broadway were paralleled in films. But, though diversionary entertainment continued to be the norm, there appeared after the war a new group of filmmakers who believed that the attractiveness of television could be countered only by offering a different kind of fare than that which had been available in the past. Therefore, they set out to provide films that would be truthful, challenging, and thoughtful as well as entertaining. Under this postwar challenge, the film came to maturity and for the first time began to be considered a serious artistic medium. But this acceptance came only gradually, for originally "art" films were shown only in minor and out-of-the-way houses. To a certain extent this is still true, but attitudes about the film have clearly altered during the past twenty years.

Meantime, changes that roughly resembled those seen in the film were underway in the theatre as well. Around 1950, a number of persons in New York began to seek alternatives to Broadway: to enlarge the range of offerings, to decentralize the theatre and to redistribute it throughout the country, and to make it a more serious artistic medium.

The first important result was the emergence of what came to be called the off-Broadway theatre. The early groups set for themselves goals that were primarily artistic. That is, they sought to present a kind of play which they considered of higher merit than those normally done on Broadway. They accepted the fact that they could not attract a mass audience but believed that it should be possible to survive by offering spectators interested in significant drama an alternative to Broadway. To keep down expenses, they found space in low-rent areas and mounted their plays so as to lessen the costs of scenery, lighting, and costumes. Many of them had to perform in buildings never intended to house theatrical productions. Consequently, whether they wished to or not, the groups had to experiment with a variety of spectator-performer relationships: arena stages, thrust stages, multiple playing areas distributed throughout the auditorium, and other arrangements. They also introduced many European playwrights, such as Eugène Ionesco,

Bertolt Brecht, and Jean Genet, to American audiences, and performed a great number of classics. In this way, the range of theatrical offerings in New York was greatly enlarged.[3]

The aims of the off-Broadway producers of the 1950s were essentially the same as those voiced by persons seeking to decentralize the theatre and to establish permanent resident companies outside of New York City. Most of these companies were founded by dedicated individuals who struggled against enormous odds and worked with extremely limited means. When they demonstrated their ability to survive, many were able to attract support from such sources as the Ford Foundation and from local contributors. As a result, since about 1960 a number of resident companies have achieved relative stability.[4]

The aims of the off-Broadway theatre of the 1950s were also essentially the same as those that have always animated the educational theatre: to present a variety of plays of high quality in such a way as to be both entertaining and stimulating. Thus, the off-Broadway theatre, the regional theatre, and the educational theatre shared similar goals, primarily artistic ones: they hoped to attract sufficient support to survive by offering good plays. Almost none of these groups of the 1950s was politically

[3] The early years of the off-Broadway theatre are treated rather thoroughly in Julia S. Price, *The Off-Broadway Theater* (New York, 1962).

[4] The resident companies outside of New York are discussed at length in Julius Novick, *Beyond Broadway: The Quest for Permanent Theatres* (New York, 1968).

oriented or deeply involved with social issues. They reflected the dominant mood of the decade: to remain detached, not to become involved. Thus, they were concerned primarily with artistic excellence rather than with commitment to a political or social position.

The regional theatre and the educational theatre are still, in this sense, institutions of the 1950s. Most still maintain the same artistic stance they took up then and most still seek to remain uncommitted to any particular extra-artistic position. This is done in part out of a conviction that art, like learning, must remain open to all points of view. But it is also done out of expediency, for both the regional and educational theatres would lose much of their support if they departed from their posture of noncommitment. This is not meant as adverse criticism but merely as a reminder that detachment is becoming increasingly difficult to maintain and that the theatre since the early 1960s has been subjected to forces quite unlike those of the 1950s, when to be detached was the norm.

The 1950s were characterized by an almost desperate attempt to maintain the *status quo*, most clearly seen in Senator Joseph McCarthy's long-unchallenged attacks on anyone who seemed to question any aspect of American tradition. It was an era when the individual sought reassurance and security and tended to avoid joining groups lest he be judged guilty by association. But this era seems also to have engendered an awareness of how vulnerable the individual is when he stands alone. Although not an

American work, the play that seems to capture best the spirit of that time is Samuel Beckett's *Waiting for Godot*,[5] with its vision of man as a derelict cast adrift in an impersonal and threatening world and subsisting on hope that is never fulfilled.

The inward-looking anxieties of the 1950s were succeeded in the 1960s by an almost diametrically opposed view—instead of detachment, commitment became the rage. Individuals banded together to create groups, who, through protests, demonstrations, and confrontations, sought to change the society which in the 1950s had created so many fears. As the demand for commitment increased, those persons or groups who refused to join one faction or another were subjected to charges of callousness, selfishness, or insensitivity to the need for reform on the one hand, or for the need to defend the tradition on the other, depending upon the persuasion of those making the charges.

The theatre did not escape these pressures. The notion that art is by its very nature essentially detached was said by many to be merely an evasion of the issues. In a statement of policy, the San Francisco Mime Theatre has declared: "We are committed to change not to Art. We have tried to cut through the aristocratic and square notion of what theatre is, and risk our egos to keep the search open for better ways of making the theatre, in con-

[5] Originally published in Paris in 1952 and in New York in 1954. It was the success of the Parisian production of *Waiting for Godot* which first attracted wide attention to Absurdist drama and began the popularity of that mode.

tent and in style, a living . . . force." [6] In much the same vein, Peter Schumann of the Bread and Puppet Theatre states, "I think the trouble with the legitimate theatre or academic theatre and so on is that they . . . have nothing to [say]." [7] Or, as Luis Valdez puts it, there is "a fantastic difference" between the aims of his company and the nonsense about scenery and lighting in academic theatre. In the academic theatre, a message "doesn't get across the seats to the audience anyway." [8] Here are statements by men who feel that the theatre should take a stand and present it forcefully in the hopes of convincing an audience of its rightness.

This demand, of course, runs directly counter to Broadway's devotion to diversionary entertainment. In fact, one stated aim of many new practitioners is to rescue the theatre from Broadway's affluent middle-class patrons and return it to all the people. They also challenge the academic theatre's emphasis upon cultural and artistic over political and social values. Such conflicting views of the theatre's function stem from widely divergent values.

No one needs to be reminded that today's world is one of conflicting values, that yawning abysses separate various groups in society. It is often argued that the dissident and radical elements are composed of only a small per-

[6] Program for Radical Theatre Festival, San Francisco State College, September, 1968, p. 12. This program gives a history of the participating companies and a transcription of a public session in which representatives of the troupes described their aims and methods.

[7] *Ibid.*, 24–25.

[8] *Ibid.*, 19.

centage of the population and that the vast majority support the traditional values of Western civilization. This estimation probably applies equally well to theatre audiences. No doubt the majority would prefer dramatic entertainment to remain in traditional paths. Most probably subscribe to the statement, "I go to the theatre to escape from my problems, not to be confronted with those of others," and do not wish to have entertainment and politics mingled, except in very small and innocuous doses.

But even if those who are seeking change are in the minority, they have made considerable impact on the public consciousness and have forced some reevaluation of the purpose of the theatre and its means. In analyzing the impact, there is a temptation to use only two categories: the new and the old. In actuality, however, there is a wide range of opinions about the theatre, just as there is about social and political problems. Consequently, among partisans on both sides there are as many differences as similarities. Some dissidents are motivated primarily by political ends, while others are more concerned about personal conduct or about social mores as they relate to love or ways of dressing and speaking. Some voice rather generalized objections to modern life, but others are very specific in their goals. What they share is a dislike for certain conventional modes of thought and behavior and a determination either to change or defy them.

Earlier it was stated that there seems to have been a revival of interest in the theatre, but this renewed awareness is probably mostly on the surface. For the majority of Americans, Broadway is "the theatre." But Broadway is rather remote from their daily lives. Since it exists in New York, it is a thing heard about more than actually experienced. The majority of those who attend the theatre in New York are not residents of that city but visitors or tourists. They go to it when they visit New York much as they might go to Disneyland when they visit Los Angeles. It is an attraction to be sampled along with the other sights and diversions. Even then, few visitors to New York venture into the off-Broadway or off-off-Broadway theatres to see some of the more adventurous productions about which they have read. For these reasons, whatever renewed interest there may be in the theatre is essentially journalistic. That is, the public has become aware of certain events in the theatre because they are newsworthy and have attracted the same kind of attention that a fad in clothing or some strange political occurrence might. The number of persons who have seen one of these newsworthy productions is few in comparison with those who have read about them. It seems doubtful that there has been any really significant increase in attendance at theatrical productions, and unless that happens the theatre will benefit little from the publicity it receives.

In fact, the theatre may eventually suffer from the attention, for what is usually picked up by the news services relates to the moral and political rather than to the artistic aspects of the theatre. And with notoriety there have come increasing demands for censorship. Throughout history public outrage has been aroused not by new artistic means but by new moral attitudes. People may be puzzled by or contemptuous of strange techniques but they usually shrug them off as hoaxes, jokes, or signs of derangement. Sometimes, however, political motives are seen lurking behind them. For example, periodically it is suggested that abstract painting is part of a Communist conspiracy. It is interesting to note that in Communist countries any tendency toward "formalism" is said to be a capitalist conspiracy. In both cases, it is assumed that anything novel must be part of a plot to undermine society. Thus, it is not surprising that when moral and political values as well as unfamiliar artistic techniques are involved, the suspicion becomes even stronger that something subversive is underway. Hence, many persons who would reject the notion that abstractionism is dangerous would favor censoring subject matter.

What has brought much of contemporary theatre its journalistic fame is not its new methods but its new values, or at any rate its seeming advocacy of behavior, language, and ideas traditionally considered unsuitable in public performances. Consequently, the most controversial aspect of the contemporary theatre is its values. The following questions illustrate the issues: Should nude actors be permitted to perform in public? Should obscenity be countenanced? Should authors be permitted to advocate political ideas that are inimical to a democratic system? Should plays be allowed to ridicule the United States? chastity? marriage? Should they be permitted to glorify the use of drugs? Should actors be allowed to perform sexual acts onstage? Where should the line be drawn? And who should draw it? We seem to be without answers to these questions, although they are very much in the public mind.

One of the productions which brought these issues most forcefully into play was *Che!* by Lennox Raphael, presented in New York in 1969. In it, Che Guevara is treated as a hero who is envied by all those who seek to thwart him. One of the envious characters, called The President, is dressed in an Uncle Sam hat and little else. Onstage, the envy seemed primarily sexually motivated, as Che became an object of desire to all the other characters. The sexual behavior was so plentiful and overt that the actors, playwright, and producer were arrested and tried on charges of public lewdness, one of the few recent instances of police action against a production in New York. All were convicted, but the decision will probably be appealed and so the ultimate outcome is uncertain. The verdict was based on the conclusion that the play had no redeeming social value and that whatever political content was intended was so underdeveloped and unclear as to be completely obscure. It read, in part, "The stage directions permitted actual sex on stage. There was no comparable testimony as to any stage direction that the political content was to be given any particular emphasis." [9] Here was a play, then, that glorified a Communist revolutionary at the expense of the United States and showed sexual acts which, as the court said,

[9] Quoted in New York *Times*, February 26, 1970, p. 31.

"ran the gamut" indiscriminately from heterosexual to homosexual. The judges put the issue and their opinions succinctly: "It cannot be said that standards of public acceptance and morality so sharply different and shocking can be established by a few commercially inspired producers who try to see how far they can go." [10] Probably the majority of persons would agree with this statement, but the truth seems to be that, as a society, America is no longer sufficiently sure of its values that it can distinguish clearly between pornography and "material with redeeming social merit," or can say with any certainty where the constitutional guarantee of freedom of speech ends and license begins. *Che!* poses the problem quite forcefully, but its solution seems far from certain.

But while the contemporary theatre may be best known to the public because of its subject matter, it has not neglected the search for new means. One major shift from earlier drama is seen in dramatic structure. In recent years, it has become increasingly difficult to find new plays that tell a clearly articulated story by first setting forth necessary information about characters and situation and then going on to develop a series of complications leading to a climax and resolution. This traditional method of ordering events has for the most part been abandoned in favor of thematic unity achieved by introducing an idea or motif and then developing variations upon it in order to increase perceptions about it. Unfortunately this kind of structure often remains ob-

[10] *Ibid.*

scure to the uninitiated and so to them the plays may seem merely confused; consequently, they are apt to feel more annoyed or outraged than enlightened.

Along with these structural patterns are found other new techniques. Language has been downgraded and its place taken over by nonverbal sound, movement, light, and a host of other devices. At least some contemporary practitioners argue that the public thinks first of all with its nerves and sinews rather than with its brain. Consequently, they feel that it is necessary to assault and shock the spectator's senses if meaningful communication is to occur.

Similarly, many argue that the spectator should not be allowed to remain comfortable in the theatre; rather, his convictions and prejudices should be attacked so that he will be forced to reassess his values. Such views are usually accompanied by political and social assumptions which the public is urged to accept. This group demands that the theatre be committed rather than detached, that it serve as a weapon for change.

What this all adds up to is an attempt to redefine the theatre, its purposes and its means. So far the attempts have made little impact on Broadway, but elsewhere they have led to greater variety in dramatic fare and theatrical method, and they have raised important fundamental questions about the theatre in general and its place in society.

TWO / The Problem of Values

Not long ago an outraged parent called the chairman of my department following the presentation of a student-written and -produced play to declare that he had not sent his daughter to the university to learn such filth—that she could do that in the gutter at home. Another parent, invited to the performance by his son, who appeared in it, professed his puzzlement over what he had seen and remarked, "I've never before felt the generation gap so keenly."

This experience reflects a fundamental conflict in today's theatre. Many of the younger practitioners see themselves as essentially honest, moral, and straightforward, and their opponents as purveyors of shopworn sentiment, discredited ideals, and meaningless clichés. On the other hand, some of those who dislike the new theatre see it as a threat to all that America stands for and as encouragement to behave and speak in ways unsuitable for public display. Furthermore, they question the claim to morality of anything that openly exhibits such behavior and employs such language. The core of this conflict is elemental: differing values, opposing views of what is truthful and

26

worthy. The issues are precisely those which underlie most divisions in contemporary society.

Hair, billed as "The American Tribal Love-Rock Musical," tries in its good-natured way to create understanding for young people who have rejected the world of their parents, and in Mom's diatribe to her son rather succinctly puts its version of the older generation's view: "We had another generation before you who went to war, went to colleges, worked for a salary . . . you're a disgrace to this country . . . just bringing attention to yourselves . . . . you're all so naive about the power structure of our civilization. The subtleties, the intricacies, . . . you don't know what's really going on . . . . what does a nineteen year old kid know? . . . I say, support our fighting, short-haired men in Vietnam." [1] Or as Dad, in the same work, says: "What's happening to our bedrock foundation of baths and underarm deodorant? How do they eat? Where do they sleep? Why do they have to be dressed like this?" [2]

Here a great many of the issues are touched on: responsibility, loyalty to country, dress and behavior, the need to face up to reality. Some of these are important, others merely symptomatic of deeper conflicts, but all reflect divisions in society and ultimately in attitudes about drama. Consequently, since questions of value are at the heart of any treatment of contemporary theatre, some of them must be raised and pursued.

[1] *Hair: The American Tribal Love-Rock Musical,* book and lyrics by Gerome Ragni and James Rado, music by Galt Mac-Dermott (New York, 1969), 109–14.
[2] *Ibid.,* 113.

Before doing so, however, it seems only fair to state some of my own assumptions. First, it appears clear to me that drama, as a product of man's consciousness, must grow out of the preoccupations of its creators. Consequently, the drama of our day necessarily reflects the conflicts evident in the world at large. Still, today as in every period there is a wide range of interests and approaches. Therefore, to talk about *the* drama of any period is necessarily to oversimplify. It is often forgotten that when we speak of Greek or Elizabethan drama we are not really discussing the average but the exceptional works, for it is only the outstanding plays that have survived and have come to be considered representative of their age. Thus the discussion that follows is not based upon some numerical norm, since most plays in nearly every age are intended merely to divert a mass audience—to make spectators forget their problems for an hour or two. Such drama usually manipulates received values and mores and rather than challenging the audience's beliefs confirms them. Most plays today, and especially those seen on Broadway and on television, are of this type. But, as in other periods, a segment of the audience and a number of playwrights now believe that drama should go beyond entertainment and reflect the preoccupations and problems of its time, however painful these may be. It is to this latter type of play that serious students normally turn when they seek to understand the drama of any period. In one's own day, it is difficult to predict which works will survive, which really represent the mainstream. Nevertheless, I think there are certain approaches in today's drama that in the future will be considered characteristic of our time. Consequently, it is primarily these that I will be discussing.

My second assumption is that all drama worthy of serious consideration attempts to reflect truth as the playwright sees it. If he distorts ordinary logic, or exaggerates action and speech, or uses strange sounds and visual effects, or adopts a diffuse organizational pattern, or resorts to obscenity and nudity, he does so in order more effectively to make a point. Consequently, behind every drama lies a playwright's conception of the human condition, and it is this vision that he seeks to convey with the most powerful means he can command. When we have difficulty understanding a play, it often, though not always, means that we have failed to comprehend the playwright's point of view.

Stemming from this assumption is a third: that differing views require differing techniques to project them. Realism, which is based on a vision of truth as that which can be objectively observed and recorded, requires a style of expression unlike that of Absurdism, which emphasizes the irrationality of experience, for irrationality cannot be projected satisfactorily through completely rational means. Consequently, content in part dictates the form and style of expression.

I make these points to emphasize the need to assume that contemporary playwrights are sincere—that their works are not intended as elaborate jokes or merely as destructive tactics, as some have suggested—and that the techniques they have adopted are determined in large part by their conceptions of reality and by their ultimate goals. Later, I will consider some of the techniques, but here I wish to examine the general outlook which underlies much of contemporary theatre.

The dominant note of contemporary drama is dissatisfaction with the past and agitation for change. There is scarcely an aspect of life that has not been questioned: politics, religion, sexual mores, the whole structure of society. Heroes from earlier generations fall almost daily. For example, President Woodrow Wilson's motives are the target of Roland Van Zandt's *Wilson in the Promise Land,* produced in New York in 1970. It "takes shape as a confrontation between the Wilson of post-Versailles, broken in mind and spirit as a result of his efforts to redeem the horror of the war with a just peace and to get the U.S. to join the League of Nations, and a troop of 'Hippies' who face him accusingly across the gulf of time. What they accuse him of is blindness to the springs of his entire career, which stemmed, they say, not from a desire to show his country 'the way to liberty and justice,' but from a messianic lust for power partially derived from a Freudian—indeed, pathological—relationship with his Presbyterian minister father. And they include in their general indictment of hypocrisy and bad faith the all-star troupe of Presidents who stand behind Wilson: Washington, Jefferson, Jackson, Lincoln, and the two Roosevelts." [3] The implications of the play are that America has become the very thing against which it

[3] From a review of the production, *Newsweek,* June 8, 1970, p. 90.

originally rebelled and that it must give up power politics and concentrate on the welfare of all mankind—although just how this ultimate goal is to be achieved is not specified. Van Zandt's play may not be typical, but it is certainly not unique among recent dramatic treatments of the American heritage.

Many observers view this questioning of traditional values as a weakening in the moral fiber of a nation grown soft with affluence and permissiveness. But this kind of questioning is not confined to America or its political spectrum, or to any single economic class or system; it is found almost everywhere. Consequently, rather than merely trying to dismiss it as misguided, subversive, or statistically insignificant, it seems more pertinent to inquire what lies behind it.

Fundamentally, we are caught in a conflict over truth. At one pole are the defenders of the *status quo*, who believe that our traditions embody values worthy of being protected from the onslaughts of those who cannot appreciate how hard-won the values have been. At the other pole are the dissidents, who tend to see these same values as essentially hypocritical disguises for dishonesty and injustice, and seek to substitute what they consider to be more truthful, honest, and equitable practices for existing ones. Since each side believes that its position represents "truth," the battle lines are laid down.

Such differences are not new, for they can be found in almost every age. The divisions have merely become sharper, more clearly defined in ours. In the period following the Second World War, it was the Absurdists who first threw down the challenge. For example, Eugène Ionesco declared his belief that the traditional ideals have become meaningless because they are now mere words used to manipulate men in a kind of conditioned stimulus-response relationship. Accused of attacking the middle class in his plays, Ionesco, after making it clear that to him "middle class" is a state of mind, replied: "For me the middle class man is just a man of slogans who no longer thinks for himself but repeats the truths that others have imposed upon him, ready made and therefore lifeless. In short [he] is a manipulated man." [4] Most of Ionesco's plays show man as a victim of slogans rather than the exemplar of values.[5]

Somewhat similarly, Friedrich Duerrenmatt in *The Visit* draws a chilling picture of the gulf between the sentiments men express and what they actually do when their selfish interests are involved. He shows townspeople declaring their outrage at being requested to kill a man, in payment for which an enormous sum of money will be distributed among them. Nevertheless, they soon begin buying on credit items which they cannot afford and eventually they acquiesce to the death and tell themselves that they have acted in the name of justice.[6]

[4] Eugène Ionesco, *Notes and Counternotes,* trans. Donald Watson (New York, 1964), 67.

[5] As, for example, in *Rhinoceros, The Bald Soprano,* and *The Chairs.*

[6] Friedrich Duerrenmatt, *The Visit,* adapted by Maurice Valency (New York, 1958). A more faithful translation has been made by Patrick Bowles (New York, 1962).

It is dissatisfaction with such hypocrisy, rather than with the traditional values themselves, that lies behind much contemporary rhetoric. Much of it insists that we cut through clichés to the substance behind them. Unfortunately, almost all deeds and statements are subject to varying interpretations and, if one is predisposed to find it, he can discover hypocrisy in them. Thus, it is easy to reexamine the past and to declare that it is not what we had supposed or to label those in power at the moment manipulators of phrases designed to mask evil or misguided motives. Consequently, much of the criticism of both the past and the present probably is unjust, although we should not leap to the opposite conclusion that it is all undeserved. Rather, let us look at some of the ways in which contemporary dramatists have rejected older standards and seek the rationale which undergirds them.

Perhaps the most obvious and certainly one of the most controversial new trends is the liberal use onstage of words long considered obscene and therefore unacceptable in public discourse. One of the most common responses is shock, but coupled with the shock is bewilderment that persons who seem to consider themselves schoolmasters to their elders would use such words. Most Americans probably consider a moral stance and obscene language basically incompatible. Herein can be seen the crux of one major conflict: the coupling of demands for peace, love, tolerance, and justice with the rejection of all that has long been thought the essence of decency, morality, and considerateness. This seeming disparity between goals and means has convinced many members of the older generation that it is the young who are hypocritical, rather than the other way around, as has often been charged. But if we are to understand the seeming contradiction, we must try to see behind the paradox.

Let us try for a moment to look dispassionately at those words labeled obscene. Most of them have been in the English vocabulary since Saxon times and most are more direct and simple than are the circumlocutions we use to say the same things. Few of the words or their meanings are unknown to us, for otherwise they could not shock us. Consequently, it seems clear that it is not the words themselves that offend us but the violation of the taboos which surround them. Used bluntly and publicly, the words become attacks upon our repressions. Therefore, the adoption of obscenity by contemporary dramatists represents in part the rejection of a refinement they consider unnecessary and which has made us refuse to employ words we all know and which are far more direct than those we normally substitute for them. There is, then, in the use of obscenity both the desire to jolt and the desire to oppose unnecessary repression. I am not seeking here either to condemn or to defend obscenity in the theatre; I wish merely to point out the emotional power that words have over us and to suggest that ultimately the judgment that a word is obscene resides in the mind of the hearer rather than inhering in the word itself. How such a word affects us depends upon the degree to which it threatens our standards. Obscenity might more properly be considered a matter of taste than of morality.

Much the same might be said about nudity and clothing. Ways of dressing or styles in hair are for the most part determined by fashion and social norms. In each era, similarity in dress is so great as to become a near-uniform, although there is always some diversity within the range established by fashion and propriety. Consequently, the abandonment of an accepted mode of dress or style of hair is another way of rejecting externally imposed standards. That nonconformists merely adopt another type of uniform is evident, but it serves nevertheless to make the divisions in society more visible. Ultimately, clothing itself can be looked upon as a form of hypocrisy, since it is worn as much to conceal as to protect the body. We were all born nude, and clothing certainly is not a natural part of us. By now someone must have said, "If man were intended by God to wear clothes, he would not have been born nude."

Explanations such as those offered here will not prevent most persons from being upset by nudity and obscenity in the theatre, for most have been taught that the public display of either is reprehensible. But, if we are asked why this should be so, we usually end by merely repeating our conviction that it is wrong. Most Americans are reared to believe that morality is (or should be) absolute—that there is a set of clearly defined principles by which life should be governed.[7] We seldom ask upon what authority these principles rest, and if challenged tend to reply that all well-brought-up persons know right from wrong and that those who refuse to live by that knowledge should be restrained. Increasingly, however, this point of view is being challenged. And, though a large proportion of the public maintains its belief in traditional morality, the philosophical foundations upon which those values rest have for more than a century been steadily eroding. As a result, fewer and fewer people now feel sufficiently certain of their standards to insist that they be enforced by society at large. Since ultimately a society can be cohesive only if it has agreed-upon values, disagreements about standards automatically lead to conflicts in society.

Since our quandary is rooted in uncertainty about values, it should be helpful to review the shifts in belief that have contributed to our dilemma. Such a survey might begin at many points, but perhaps the most fruitful is the nineteenth century, for it was the conditions created by the Industrial Revolution that motivated most of the crucial changes.

With the establishment of factories in the nineteenth century the whole pattern of daily life was drastically altered. Rather than working at home, as had been usual,

[7] Perhaps I am wrong to declare that most Americans believe in an absolute standard of morality. Nevertheless, it seems to me that most youngsters are taught an unshaded moral code and that much contemporary disillusionment stems from an unwillingness to accept that the moral standard varies according to the situation. Any deviation is apt to raise the specter of hypocrisy.

laborers were brought together in factories. One consequence was rapid urbanization, with which came a host of problems, most clearly seen in the vast slums that grew up in industrial towns. Unfortunately, these challenges came at a time when governments were little inclined to deal with them. In Europe, the memories of the French Revolution and the Reign of Terror had led rulers to adopt policies designed to see that such events never happened again. Consequently, when agitation about urban problems began, governments failed to distinguish between legitimate demands for social reform and revolutionary politics. Since in most countries voting rights were restricted to property owners, the working classes were generally disenfranchised while the middle and upper classes were little inclined to vote for changes which would benefit the workers. An impasse was reached and, not surprisingly, the hard line adopted by European governments eventually led to the very thing they most feared—rebellion. The first wave of uprisings came in 1830 and a second, more intense one between 1845 and 1850. Although most were put down, by 1850 it had become evident that more democratic political systems were needed and that numerous pressing social problems were crying out for solution.[8] No doubt this situation explains why dramatists in the late nineteenth century for the first time began to treat the

[8] The social and political conditions of this period are treated at length in Jacques Droz, *Europe Between Revolutions, 1815–1848*, trans. Robert Baldick (New York, 1967), and Jacob L. Talmon, *Romanticism and Revolt: Europe, 1815–48* (New York, 1967).

problems of the lower classes with the seriousness formerly reserved for the middle and upper classes.

Here, however, I am interested primarily in the disillusionment with the past that accompanied the rebellions. Earlier outlooks were declared bankrupt and more truthful ones sought. Of the many suggestions, the most influential was that set forth by Auguste Comte, the founder of sociology, who proclaimed the great task of his age to be the application of precise observation, hypothesis, and analysis to social phenomena so that the causes of problems might be determined and the effects controlled.[9] Thus, Comte sought in science the key to the problems then plaguing mankind, and in general the major thinkers of the late nineteenth century followed his lead.

The intense interest in science brought rapid developments in almost every field and the creation of several new ones. For example, psychology was separated from philosophy and soon was suggesting novel conclusions about human motivations. Anthropology, archaeology, and geology accumulated evidence which challenged many traditional beliefs, several considered articles of religious faith. For example, it had long been assumed that the world was only 6,000 years old (a figure arrived at by counting the generations enumerated in the Bible). Thus, when geologists began to realize the truly ancient nature of the earth and when archaeologists uncovered

[9] Auguste Comte's philosophical position was set forth in *Positive Philosophy* (5 vols., 1830–42) and his suggestions for implementing a program in *Positive Polity* (4 vols., 1851–54).

human fossils hundreds of thousands of years old, the Bible itself seemed under attack, and science was increasingly assigned the role of skeptic about all traditional beliefs.[10]

The greatest impact was made, however, by Charles Darwin's *Origin of the Species,* published in 1859. In this work, Darwin set out to explain how the various species came into existence and how and why they changed. His explanation had two essential parts. First, he argued that all life forms have evolved from a common ancestry. This notion was not original, having been suggested by the ancient Greeks, but Darwin, unlike his predecessors, supplied an immense amount of evidence to support his contentions. Second, he argued that evolution took place through a process of natural selection— the ability of a species to adapt to environmental circumstances—or the "survival of the fittest." Reduced to its essentials, Darwin's theory sought to explain all biological phenomena in terms of heredity and environment.

The implications of Darwin's ideas are many, although he himself was not aware of them all. First, they greatly reduce, perhaps even eliminate, the role of God or Providence (which had played a major part in almost all

[10] The history of geology, archaeology, and anthropology are treated in many books, among them: F. D. Adams, *The Birth and Development of the Geological Sciences* (Baltimore, 1938) ; H. R. Hays, *From Ape to Angel: An Informal History of Social Anthropology* (New York, 1958) ; J. O. Brew (ed.) , *One Hundred Years of Anthropology* (Cambridge, Mass., 1968) ; G. E. Daniel, *Origins and Growth of Archeology* (Harmondsworth, England, 1967) ; and K. W. Marek, *Gods, Graves, and Scholars: The Story of Archeology,* trans. E. B. Garside (New York, 1951) .

earlier views) . Darwin's argument that all life forms have evolved from a common ancestry contradicts the story of creation as given in the Bible (at least if interpreted literally). Furthermore, if causality can be reduced to heredity and environment, divine intervention in human affairs is unnecessary and unlikely. Consequently, attention is directed away from the supernatural to the purely natural. At the same time, man's place in the universe is seriously altered. In Biblical terms, man is a deliberate creation, the superior of other earthly creatures, over whom he has been given command by God. But in Darwinian terms, man is an accidental product of a natural process; he is absorbed into nature as merely another animal rather than, as in the Biblical view, being somehow superior to (or an exception to) animalistic nature.

Perhaps most important, the scheme of causality summed up in the terms *heredity* and *environment* led to a semischizophrenic view which has plagued society since Darwin's time. On the one hand, if everything that happens can be explained by hereditary and environmental factors, then men should be able to change society by manipulating causes. In other words, if a particular result is desired, it should be attainable if the proper conditions are created. Thus, there has been in modern thought an element of utopianism—the notion that if only those in a position to make decisions would make the right ones an ideal society could be created. This idea is much in evidence today, for it is often implied that were it not for the selfishness and shortsightedness of those in power, there might be not merely a more just society but a society free from injustice.

On the other hand, the emphasis upon heredity and environment also tends to depict the individual as a victim of circumstances beyond his control. Obviously no one has control over his heredity and little over his environment during the years when his personality is being shaped. Can he be considered the architect of his own fate if he is molded by forces beyond his control? The implications of this question for morality are enormous. Can a man be blamed for his actions if they are determined by conditions over which he has no power? Taken to its logical extreme, such determinism means that whatever a man does, he must do. The gradual acceptance of the view of man-as-victim has led to many changes in legal doctrine and moral values, for it has come to seem inhumane to impose harsh punishments on those who have been forced into crime or immorality by circumstances. Consequently, punishments for crimes have altered markedly during the past century. On the other hand, the Puritan ethic, which has dominated American thought, teaches that transgressors should be punished and that to spare the rod is to spoil the child. Caught between the urge to understand and the urge to be strict, we vacillate. Which should be given priority —the punishment of wrongdoing, or the correction of the social conditions that lead to wrongdoing? The alternatives constitute one of the polar divisions of our time.

Another significant result of the nineteenth-century

faith in science was skepticism about religion. Those who wished to promote a systematic approach to the solution of social ills were almost forced into a conflict with religious faith, for Christianity had always depicted the world as an imperfect place that had to be endured on the path to eternity. Since perfection lay in God and the next world, the ills of this world tended to be viewed as inevitable, and thus the stoical endurance of hardship and deprivations was often considered proof of one's worthiness for eternal salvation. Consequently, the success of social reform depended in part upon the rejection of such views.

Furthermore, with the fervor for science came the urge to concentrate attention on those questions that can be answered with certainty through the scientific method—that is, through hypothesis, analysis, observation, and proof. Some writers began to argue that only those things established by such a process can legitimately be called true, for all else really falls into the realm of opinion or faith. This argument automatically placed religion, based as it is on faith, outside the realm of truth, just as it did morality, for the application of the scientific method to ethical systems only demonstrates that values inevitably are subjective and beyond verification.

Thus, a breach was made in the fortress of morality. The validity of the Bible had been seriously challenged by Darwin's theories and by a series of scientific discoveries, just as zealous advocates of the scientific method had relegated all religion to the category of opinion. Morality could not fail to be affected, for in the Western world it has almost always derived its sanctions from religion. God (or some absolute power and judge) has almost always been considered the ordainer of the moral system. Consequently, to question morality was to question God and vice versa. If one weakens faith in God, one also undermines the absolute basis for morality, and, if no new faith is found to replace it, one moral system begins to seem as truthful as another, for all moral judgments must be made in relation to some standard, and if the standard is wholly subjective then so will be the ethical system based upon it.

The implications for morality of nineteenth-century developments were not immediately felt; in fact, they were not fully apparent until after World War II. It was probably Jean-Paul Sartre who best formulated the concepts that were to exert the greatest influence on present-day thought. Since the 1930s, Sartre has been arguing that there is no God or any system of values ordained by a supernatural or absolute power, and consequently that all ideals are man-made. Since man owes no allegiance to any superior power, he is free. But this freedom is a terrible burden, for it demands of each person that he choose his own values instead of accepting those handed to him by others. Once having chosen, man is moral and truly himself only to the degree that he abides by his choices, regardless of the opposition he encounters.[11] It is this Sartrean insistence upon choos-

11 Jean-Paul Sartre's position is set forth in several books and essays. Among those most readily available are *Being and Nothingness: An Essay on Phenomenological Ontology*, translated and

ing for oneself that informs so many of today's events.

Sartre's philosophical position was greatly strengthened by another postwar occurrence, one intended to have an opposite effect: the Nuremberg war-crimes trials. These trials were based on the premise that there is a set of moral principles which takes precedence over man-made laws and national policies. German officials were convicted for refusing to disobey German laws and because they did not defy governmental demands. No doubt implicit in these trials was the notion that law should conform to moral principle, but they also clearly implied that each man must decide when his moral convictions are in conflict with the law and that convictions take precedence. Pushed to its logical extreme, this means that each individual should decide which laws he will obey and which he will defy.

Sartre's ideas are crucial in still other ways to an understanding of postwar drama. To him, the universe is impersonal, for, since it is not governed by any god, there is no rational order behind existence. It is up to man, then, to bring some order to life if he can. It was essentially these notions that Albert Camus had in mind when he labeled the human condition "absurd." According to Camus, absurdity results from man's perception of the disparity between his hopes and desires and the impersonal and irrational universe into which he

---

with an introduction by Hazel E. Barnes (New York, 1956) ; *Literary and Philosophical Essays*, trans. Annette Michelson (New York, 1955) ; and *Of Human Freedom*, ed. Wade Basken (New York, 1966) .

has been thrown. Man's position is absurd because his inborn desire for order is completely irrational in a universe which is itself devoid of purpose.[12] It was these twin themes of impersonality and irrationality which informed most Absurdist drama of the 1950s. It took many forms. Samuel Beckett was most concerned with metaphysical questions about man's place in the universe.[13] Other playwrights were preoccupied with political and social impersonality. Duerrenmatt comments on man's relationship to the state in the contemporary world: "The state today . . . cannot be envisioned, for it is anonymous and bureaucratic. . . . Any . . . petty government official or policeman better represents our world than [does] a senator or president. Today art can only embrace the victim, if it can reach man at all; it can no longer come close to the mighty. Creon's secretaries close Antigone's case." [14] In Ionesco's plays, absurdity is conceived primarily in social terms. In *Rhinoceros*, for example, he shows how men become so conditioned to demands for conformity that they willingly turn into rhinoceroses because everyone else is doing so.[15]

[12] Camus sets forth these ideas most forcefully in "The Myth of Sisyphus," now readily available in English in Albert Camus, *The Myth of Sisyphus and Other Essays*, trans. Justin O'Brien (New York, 1955), 1–138.

[13] As in *Waiting for Godot, Endgame, Play*, and various other works, both dramatic and nondramatic.

[14] Friedrich Duerrenmatt, "Problems in the Theatre," in *European Theories of the Drama*, edited by Barrett H. Clark and revised by Henry Popkin (New York, 1965), 316.

[15] *Rhinoceros* was written in 1958, first performed in 1959, and published in an English translation by Derek Prouse in Eugène Ionesco, *Plays* (7 vols.; London, 1958–68), IV, 3–107.

Thus, although the Absurdists viewed man from many angles, their conclusions were always much the same: man inhabits a godless universe and therefore his attempts to construct systems of morality or standards of conduct have no absolute foundation. Because there is no point of fixity, all systems are ultimately irrational. Man is cut off from his fellow creatures, for they can offer him no comfort or security and are in fact more apt either to destroy or dehumanize than to assist him. The major mood of Absurdist drama is anxiety, a feeling of being at the mercy of irrational forces which are beyond comprehension, of fear for the loss of personal identity. Furthermore, the Absurdists seem to question whether it is worth the effort to act, since all actions are equally meaningless. They explore the human condition but seem paralyzed by what they find.[16]

The passive contemplation which typified the 1950s gave way in the 1960s to a quite different mood. Again, Sartre provides one key to the change. The absurdists tended to accept only that part of Sartre's view which declares that the world is irrational and that moral systems have no foundation in absolutes. They ignored his conclusions about what man should do in the face of this condition: find a meaningful moral stance and act resolutely on it. Thus, Sartre was concerned primarily with providing a rationale for individual morality and action. On the other hand, one of the major political lessons of

16 A good general survey of Absurdism can be found in Martin Esslin, *The Theatre of the Absurd* (rev. ed.; Garden City, N.Y., 1969).

the 1950s, brought home forcefully by Senator Joseph McCarthy's tactics, was the vulnerability of the individual. It took Dr. Martin Luther King's advocacy of civil disobedience to demonstrate that the individual can find strength by joining with others to achieve a common goal. Sartre's notion that each man must create his own standards and act firmly on them was thus transferred to group action.

As the focus shifted from the individual to the group in the 1960s, drama changed accordingly. No longer were characters drawn as individuals but were treated instead as representatives of specific groups or of varying attitudes toward a problem. In another context, but quite pertinently, Sartre has said: "We are not greatly concerned with psychology. We are not searching for the right 'word' which will reveal the whole unfolding of a passion, nor yet the 'act' which will seem most life-like and inevitable to the audience . . . . our theatre would betray its mission if it portrayed individual personalities, even if they were as universal types as a miser, a misanthrope, a deceived husband." [17] Or, as Luis Valdez has said, "Who responds [nowadays] to Tennessee Williams or Arthur Miller picking his liver apart?" [18]

In recent years drama has steadily replaced the traditional concern for the individual with others—ideas, issues, groups. It is now widely believed that the mark

[17] Jean-Paul Sartre, "Forgers of Myths," in Clark (ed.), *European Theories of the Drama*, 402.
[18] Program for Radical Theatre Festival, San Francisco State College, September, 1968, p. 20.

of a responsible person is his willingness to take a stand —and consequently more and more people are taking stands. Today we have taken and continue to take up positions on almost every conceivable issue: war, peace, national policy, economics, poverty, racial relations, sexual mores, dress and behavior, and art.[19]

All of these have found their way into drama. And, as the notions that the past has been mistaken and that our society is repressive have gained increasing acceptance, there has been a tendency deliberately to choose subjects previously considered unacceptable either because of morality or ideology. Predictably, some productions merely exploit sensationalism; it is often difficult to know when dramatists are expressing sincere convictions and when they are merely capitalizing on the current tolerance of the daring and erotic.

Those persons in our society who still subscribe to the

[19] The most forceful challenges to traditional ideas are those posed by the New Left. Many of these were derived from such works as Herbert Marcuse, *Eros and Civilization* (New York, 1964) and *One Dimensional Man* (New York, 1964) ; R. D. Laing, *The Divided Self* (London, 1960) and *The Politics of Experience* (London, 1967) ; and Norman O. Brown, *Life Against Death* (New York, 1959) and *Love's Body* (New York, 1966) . Among the most important of the many ideas espoused by the New Left are: (1) that Freud's notion that the "pleasure principle" must be kept in check by the "reality principle" is mistaken; (2) that, since the new proletariat, composed of engineers and technicians, are the chief supporters of middle-class values, some social ills will be overcome only by the abandonment of democratic procedures and only through the efforts of students and minority groups; and (3) that happiness depends upon freedom from restraints and from competitiveness.

idea that morality is near-absolute—and there are a great number of them—find it difficult to grant that any deviations from traditional values should be tolerated. But there is no easy answer to the problem of values. Much contemporary drama is boring, a lot of it is pretentious, and the majority of it, like the majority of drama in any period, is ultimately insignificant. So, one would probably be justified in dismissing most of it as unimportant. Nevertheless, much of it is sincerely seeking to illuminate our world for us, to inspire in us a desire for a better life. If we look beyond the often-objectionable surface, we will see that in much of it there is an almost childlike desire to believe in the goodness of man. Much of it might more rightly be condemned for naiveté than for obscenity.

Many questions of value, both in drama and in life, ultimately come down to what we think of man's potential. The conservative tends to see man as a creature who easily goes astray and who needs to be kept in check through the enforcement of rather clearly defined standards which have been established over a long period of time. He sees man as relatively static, much the same in every period, and in need of a system that will insure that his energies are properly channeled. He does not approve of attacks on traditional values. The liberal tends to see man as improvable rather than as static. Thus, he believes that the system must constantly be examined and adjusted so that man may achieve his highest potential.

Traditionally, we have set up the conservative and liberal views as polar. But increasingly we must now contend as well with the radical, or, more accurately, the utopian view, which is based on the premise, not that man is static or improvable, but that he is perfectible—that we could have a perfect society, absolute love, freedom, and justice if only those in a position to act would take the right steps. This generalized utopian view is well summed up by a song from *Hair*: "Exanaplanetooch, a planet in another galaxy . . . . a planet where the air is pure, the river waters crystal bright . . . total beauty, total health, every man's an artist, and a scientist-philosopher, no government, and no police, no wars, no crime, no hate, just happiness and love, fulfillment of each man's potential and ambition and ever-widening horizons." [20] As a vision (or nostalgic picture) of an ideal world, it is nearly perfect, but it is a vision which, if used as a yardstick by which to measure this world, can easily lead to the conviction that if what we have is not perfect or is not perfectible, it should be destroyed. Thus, violence may seem the quickest road to an ideal society.

What one thinks about the theatre today depends upon many things, but most importantly upon one's moral values and upon one's conceptions of man and his potential. Thus, here I have been concerned primarily with values in the world at large rather than in specific plays. But, if contemporary drama is to be understood, it must be seen as a reflection of its world. If much of today's theatre is disturbing, it is merely symptomatic of larger

[20] *Hair*, 191–92.

issues. Given our current divergent views on morality, we have only two courses open to us: reasonable tolerance or forcible repression. The only possible way we could achieve uniformity of standards would be through repressive force. Ultimately the only answer lies in healing the divisions within our society so that we may arrive at sufficiently strong and commonly held beliefs that both dissent and repression seem irrelevant.

THREE / Changing Conceptions of Unity

Much of the confusion surrounding today's drama can be attributed to structural devices, for the uninitiated spectator often is left confused by a jumble of seemingly unrelated elements. Consequently, rather than perceiving any overall significance in a work, he frequently comes away remembering a few moments—all too often those that impressed him because of radical ideas, bold behavior, or obscene language. Thus, structural patterns contribute to the suspicion that plays are attacking traditional values even when the authors are affirming deepfelt ethical principles. Therefore, novel structure contributes to anxieties about the contemporary theatre almost as much as do novel values. It is these changing conceptions of unity— of structural wholeness—that I wish to examine here, for it is the failure to perceive the whole that leads so many audiences to misinterpret the parts.

As an example of a contemporary play, let us look briefly at Adrienne Kennedy's *The Owl Answers*, a work with several layers of meaning and in which the identity of characters shifts rapidly. The author describes the protagonist as "She who is Clara Passmore who is the Virgin

Mary who is the Bastard who is the Owl." Following the
list of characters, this explanation is given: "The characters change slowly back and forth into and out of themselves, leaving some garment from their previous selves
upon them." The setting is "A New York subway is the
Tower of London is a Harlem Hotel Room is St. Peter's."
The text begins with a lengthy stage direction ending
with this passage: "Four people enter from different directions. They are Shakespeare, William the Conqueror,
Chaucer, and Anne Boleyn, but too they are strangers
entering a subway on a summer night, too they are guards
in the Tower of London. Their lines throughout the play
are not spoken specifically by one person but by all or
part of them." [1] From these quotations it should be clear
that in *The Owl Answers* past and present flow together
and overlap, that several places are suggested simultaneously, that characters merge and separate, that there is
a literary, a historical, a religious, and a contemporary
plane of reference. (In fact, there are other planes as
well, but these are the most obvious ones.) An interesting and complex play, it can also easily be a confusing
one because it is organized primarily through association
and suggestion. I am not interested here so much in the
play's merit as in its departure from traditional dramatic
structure (that is, from the cause-to-effect relationship
among incidents) .

[1] The text of Adrienne Kennedy's play *The Owl Answers* may
be found in *New American Plays*, ed. William M. Hoffman (New
York, 1968) , II, 249–68. The passages quoted here are from pp.
250–52.

Using the traditional method, the playwright sets up in the opening scenes all the necessary conditions—the situation, the desires and motivations of the characters —out of which the later events develop. The goals of one character come into conflict with those of another, or two conflicting desires within the same character may lead to a crisis. Attempts to surmount the obstacles make up the substance of the play, each scene growing logically out of those which have preceded it. This is the structure that typifies most drama from the time of the Greeks to the modern era. In the *Poetics*, Aristotle describes with admirable simplicity the logical whole which was his ideal, as well as that of dramatists in most later periods: "A whole is that which has a beginning, a middle, and an end. A beginning is that which of necessity does not follow anything, while something by nature follows or results from it. On the other hand, the end is that which naturally, of necessity, or most generally, follows something else but nothing follows it. . . . Therefore, those who would arrange plots well must not begin just anywhere in the story nor end at just any point, but they must adhere to the criteria here laid down." Aristotle goes on to say, "The different parts of the action must be so related to each other that if any part is changed or taken away the whole will be altered and disturbed. For anything whose presence or absence makes no discernible difference is no essential part of the whole." [2]

[2] Aristotle, *Poetics*, trans. Ingram Bywater (Oxford, 1909). The first passage is from Chap. 7, the second from Chap. 8.

What Aristotle is championing here, of course, is unity of *action*—a complete, whole, and fully developed story, with all the incidents clearly and logically related to each other in such a way that one seems to grow out of another. It is the kind of unity favored by Sophocles, Plautus, Shakespeare, Molière, Ibsen, and a host of lesser dramatists.

Although the cause-to-effect arrangement of incidents has been favored by dramatists of the past, it is, as Miss Kennedy's play demonstrates, not the only way of organizing drama. In fact, the majority of nonrealistic playwrights in the modern era have abandoned the cause-to-effect organization in favor of a thematic arrangement, or in Aristotelian terms, a unity of thought. In this kind of organization, scenes are linked because they relate to some central idea, motif, or argument. When a play is unified through thought, the structure is apt to be loose, often giving the effect of randomness, because the incidents are not causally related. In fact, successive incidents may involve completely different characters and lines of action, so long as they relate in some way to the central idea. Since in this kind of play the focus is on theme, arguments, or issues, the characters and incidents are of secondary importance. They need be developed only enough and as required to illustrate thought. In the traditional play, on the other hand, though it is not neglected, thought is subordinated to action by making it an aspect of character. In other words, ideas come in only as they are voiced by the characters and as they motivate the characters to act. Thus, thought contributes

causally. That is, one event *follows* another but does not necessarily *grow out of* it. And, as Aristotle points out, "it makes a great deal of difference whether the incidents happen because of what has preceded or merely after it." [4] *The Chairs* is a relatively simple example of thematic development, for in it the time is continuous, the place unchanging, and the characters few.

A more complex example can be seen in *Hair*.[5] Here the characters are numerous, although few are given names, and the place is indefinite, although it is described in the stage directions as "New York City, mostly the East Village." There is no through-line of action, except perhaps the tenuous one revolving around whether Claude will burn his draft card or accept induction. Some relationships between characters are established but not for the purpose of telling a continuous story. As a whole, the work is a collection of "moments" which together seek to express the anxieties, aspirations, and ideals of youth and to declare opposition to war and to many social conventions and values. It illustrates, perhaps in the extreme, that there are marked similarities between musical compositions and drama unified through thought, since in both a theme is introduced and then variations improvised upon it.

There are, then, two principal methods—the cause-to-effect arrangement of incidents, and the grouping of

[4] Aristotle, *Poetics*, Chap. 10.
[5] *Hair: The American Tribal Love-Rock Musical*, book and lyrics by Gerome Ragni and James Rado, music by Galt MacDermott (New York, 1969).

material around idea—which have been used most often by dramatists. There are other ways of organizing drama, but, since they are normally used only in conjunction with one of the methods described here, they are secondary and need not concern us.

Keeping these notions about organization in mind, I would like to turn now to another thesis: the method used by a playwright in unifying his action is determined in part by his conception of the world in which he lives— the degree to which he finds his world rational, logical, and knowable. Prior to the modern era, playwrights in almost all periods seem to have been convinced that the world is ruled by supernatural powers who are essentially rational—that is, that the world is presided over by a god who has some plan in mind which gives order to the universe. Obviously, conceptions of this divine power have varied from one time to another, for the notions of Greeks and Romans about the gods differed from those of the Christians, who came to dominate Europe after the fall of the Roman Empire. But, though conceptions of the nature of divinity changed, there was no drastic alteration in the belief that this is a universe given direction by some consciousness which lies behind it and rules over it. Thus, the same basic assumptions underlie the plays of Sophocles and Shakespeare despite their separation in time and place. Because they assume that the world has direction and purpose, both authors use the cause-to-effect arrangement of incidents as the primary means of organizing their plays. In their works, events happen in part because the characters are particular kinds of people who respond in particular ways to events, and the outcome is a result of character and event working in combination. In *King Lear,* everything that happens is a direct outcome of conditions established in the beginning scenes: that is, Lear's decision to divide his kingdom, his hasty disinheritance of Cordelia and his abdication of power to his two evil daughters, Goneril and Regan. As Lear comes to realize his mistake, he moves from helplessness to madness, and finally to recovery. By the time he dies, he has come to understand both himself and his world much more fully than he did in the beginning. But while this action progresses on the human level, there is always evident in the background a divine order, which is constantly evoked through the metaphorical language and whose presence is felt in the storm and especially in the restoration of order to human affairs. At its conclusion, *King Lear* is pervaded by a sense of the interaction between the natural and supernatural worlds and with the reminder that man cannot disrupt the order ordained by God without suffering dire consequences.

The same relationship between the human and divine is found in Sophocles' plays as well, although the specific devices used to convey it differ markedly. This relationship was to continue until the nineteenth century, although under Neoclassicism it was to become overly self-conscious and schematized into the doctrine of poetic justice. In the seventeenth and eighteenth centuries, dramatists were expected not merely to copy life but to reveal its ideal moral patterns. Since God was thought to be both all-powerful and just, drama was expected to show wickedness punished and virtue rewarded. Those instances in life in which injustice seemed to prevail were said to be a part of God's plan, which at times may escape human understanding but which inevitably makes justice prevail. Therefore, apparent departures from justice should be avoided by the dramatist, for playwrights should depict truth, which is inseparable from morality and justice.[6]

Adherence to the doctrine of poetic justice produced, by modern standards, extremely oversimplified views of human experience. The plays of the eighteenth century are organized to show that the outcome—reward for the virtuous, punishment for the wicked—is the direct result of incidents shown or choices made in the drama. Thus, there is a clear cause-to-effect arrangement.

The Neoclassical doctrine of poetic justice was inherited by nineteenth-century melodrama. In melodrama, no matter how devious the villain or how helpless the protagonist, evil is foiled, often by what seems direct intervention from Divine Providence, for in many plays the villain gets his just deserts because some natural disaster engulfs him at the moment of seeming triumph. Many melodramas of the nineteenth century were episodic in structure, but they always demonstrated the justness of the universe.

This vision of a just universe was seriously challenged in the late nineteenth century by the growing interest

[6] For a fuller treatment of this view, see Oscar G. Brockett, *The Theatre* (New York, 1969), 171–74.

in science. In drama, the new outlook found its expression in Realism and Naturalism. Dramatists associated with these movements deemphasized the notion of divine causation. It was not so much that they were atheistic as concerned with purely human causation. In that era, advocates of a scientific approach suggested that many problems had not been solved in the past because things not understood had too often been attributed to "the will of God." They suggested, therefore, that it would be better to ignore the supernatural and seek diligently into the natural causes of human problems. But downgrading the supernatural did not mean downgrading the view that this is a rational universe. Rather, the scientific outlook was predicated upon the notion that this is a wholly comprehensible world if we will approach it systematically through observation, analysis, hypothesis, and conclusion. In drama, rather than undermining the cause-to-effect arrangement of incidents, the new outlook strengthened it. No movements have laid so much stress on cause-to-effect organization as have Realism and Naturalism.

The increased emphasis upon rigorous logic in drama is first seen clearly in the 1870s and 1880s, in Henrik Ibsen's prose plays, usually considered the beginning of modern drama. *A Doll's House* demonstrates the organizational pattern that has been typical of realistic drama since that time.[7] Before the play opens, Nora Helmer,

[7] The text of Henrik Ibsen's play *A Doll's House* is available in many editions. Perhaps the most authoritative is that in *Ibsen*, trans. and ed. James Walter McFarlane (7 vols.; London, 1961), V, 197–343.

unaware of the law, has forged her father's signature in order to borrow money from the disreputable Nils Krogstad so that she may take her husband to Italy, where he can recuperate from a critical illness. When the play opens, her husband, Torvald, has recovered and is a respected bank manager. The family, which includes two small children, seems the epitome of happiness and respectability. The first act is devoted to establishing the characters and the events that have occurred before the play begins. Out of this opening, everything thereafter grows logically and with seeming inevitability.

Scarcely has the play started before the past begins to catch up with Nora, as Krogstad tries to blackmail her. Though frightened, Nora is convinced that Torvald will praise her for her initiative in saving his life. But when he learns of her actions, Torvald, concerned only with the threat to his position, denounces Nora as monstrous and declares her unfit to rear his children. Horrified, Nora realizes that she has always been treated as a plaything rather than as a partner. She leaves her husband and children, determined to achieve her potential as a human being.

There is in this play no suggestion of divine justice. Rather, Nora is depicted as the product of a society which treats women as playthings, keeping them ignorant of business and other affairs that would permit them to stay out of the clutches of men such as Krogstad. Similarly, Torvald is a product of a society which values respectability and position more than it does a wife's love. Rather than demonstrating an interaction between the divine and the human, *A Doll's House* shows merely an interaction between environment, character, and action. Both causes and effects are clearly defined; logic and order are transformed into dramatic structure.

Although Ibsen's plays, in one sense, mark the beginning of modern drama, in another they mark the culmination of earlier trends, since, except for Realism and Naturalism, modern movements have tended to abandon the cause-to-effect arrangement of incidents in favor of unity of theme. Before the modern developments are examined, however, it will be helpful to make some additional distinctions. Up to this point, unity through thought or theme has been treated as though all plays unified in this manner were similar. There are, however, at least two major kinds of drama which use this arrangement and these need to be separated before we continue.

First, there is the essentially didactic play in which the episodes are chosen to illustrate an argument and add up to a demonstration. The authors of such plays may believe just as firmly that this is a rational world as does the playwright who organizes his works through cause-to-effect. They at least give the appearance of believing their audiences sufficiently rational to recognize the validity of the demonstrations offered them. The oldest plays that use this method are the ancient Greek comedies written by Aristophanes in the fifth century B.C. In those works, Aristophanes sets forth a "happy idea" about how to bring about some desired result, such as an end to war. There is a debate over the merits of the proposal; the idea is then adopted and a series of scenes shows the happy results. The plays mingle fantasy, commentary on politics, drama, and other aspects of contemporary Athenian life, and a great deal of buffoonery to create an exaggerated comic world which argues strongly for the acceptance of the idea being championed. Medieval morality plays are also designed to provide a demonstration, but, unlike Aristophanes' comedies, they are serious plays which show the necessity of following the Christian way of life.

Still, few examples of this type of play can be found prior to the modern period. In the twentieth century, however, this kind of organization has become common. It can be seen in the Expressionist drama written between about 1910 and 1925, and, above all, in Bertolt Brecht's epic theatre. Brecht believed that the theatre should make the audience face issues, weigh evidence, and transfer what it had decided to problems outside the theatre. Thus, while like the Realists he wanted to better society, Brecht believed that they had erred by imitating reality so closely that stage illusion had become for the spectators a distraction from real issues, since it implied that the problems had been solved in the plays themselves.[8] Consequently, Brecht adopted a number of devices—songs, projections, direct address to the audience, visible lighting and stage machinery, and so on—

[8] Bertolt Brecht's writings about the theatre have been collected in *Brecht on Theatre,* trans. John Willett (New York, 1964). Of these, the most authoritative is "A Short Organum for the Theatre," 179–205.

to keep the audience aware that it was in a theatre and that, while what it saw was related to life, it could not substitute for action outside the theatre.

In Brecht's play *The Good Woman of Setzuan*,[9] three gods come down to earth in search of a good person. Because of the general indifference to them, however, they are forced to accept lodgings with a prostitute, Shen Te. They decide that she is the good person they have been seeking, and when they leave remind her to remain good. She is skeptical about her ability to do so, saying: "I'd like to be good, it's true, but there's the rent to pay. . . . How is it done? Even breaking a few of your commandments, I can hardly manage." One of the gods replies, "That's not our sphere. We never meddle with economics." This, of course, sets the problem that Brecht has in mind—the relationship between morality and the economic system. How can we be good if we are forced by the system to prostitute ourselves in order to survive?

Eventually the gods give Shen Te a sum of money, and the remainder of the play shows her struggles to live by the gods' commandments. But when others find out that she has money, they almost overwhelm her. To save herself, she assumes a disguise. As Shui Ta, her cousin, she becomes an exploiting capitalist, forcing the others to work for her. Eventually, however, she is overcome by circumstances which arise because of her innate goodness, and the gods arrive just in time to rescue her. But

[9] The text of *The Good Woman of Setzuan* is readily available in English in *Parables for the Theatre: Two Plays by Bertolt Brecht*, trans. Eric Bentley (Minneapolis, 1961).

the rescue is only temporary, for they leave her once more just where she was at the beginning—with injunctions to be good. Thus, there is no resolution to the play. But this is intentional on Brecht's part. In an epilogue, he asks: "How could a better ending be arranged?/ Could one change people? Can the world be changed?" Brecht clearly implies that the economic system should be changed, but he avoids saying so outright. Rather, in the final lines, he states: "It is for you to find a way, my friends,/ To help good men arrive at happy ends./ *You* write the happy ending to the play./ There must, there must, there's got to be a way."

It should be obvious from this summary that *The Good Woman of Setzuan* has a connected story. But it may not be obvious that it is not arranged in a cause-to-effect manner. The injunction to be good provides a starting point, but thereafter the way in which the attempt and failure are shown is largely arbitrary, for it does not grow out of character or environment but is dictated by the needs of the argument. It is important to note that Brecht avoids directly stating any message. Thus, although he is a didactic playwright, he chooses to work through parables, that is, through stories which, though not specifically about immediate problems, parallel and illuminate them.

Brecht's method has been extremely influential on recent drama. A great many contemporary plays are didactic, seeking to make us think about specific issues or situations and come to some conclusions or take some action on them. Like Brecht's, however, a contemporary drama often does not work directly, but uses instead a parablelike story as a medium of argument.

Before examining contemporary practice more specifically, however, let us look at the second type of play organized around theme—that is, the play based on the assumption that the universe is unknowable, illogical, or mysterious. Such works show *what* happens, but do not clarify *why* it happens, beyond the general notion that life itself is mysterious. A good example is Maurice Maeterlinck's *Pélléas and Mélisande*,[10] usually considered the finest Symbolist drama of the late nineteenth century. It tells of an ill-starred love between Mélisande and her husband's brother, Pélléas. They fall in love against their wills and eventually die because of it. But this story is developed only obliquely and the various episodes serve primarily to evoke a mood of doom and mystery. Maeterlinck seems to suggest that, like sheep being led to the slaughter, we are all driven by forces beyond our comprehension. In this play, there is sequence but not causality. That is, one event follows another but is not caused by it. This was to be true as well of Surrealist and Absurdist drama.

In such plays can be seen a characteristic feature of much modern art: the juxtaposition of elements whose relationships are unclear.[11] The effect is discontinuity—

[10] Maurice Maeterlinck, *Pélléas and Mélisande*, trans. Richard Hovey (New York, 1896).

[11] A very penetrating discussion of this point can be found in Roger Shattuck, *The Banquet Years: The Origins of the Avant-Garde in France, 1885 to World War I* (rev. ed.; New York, 1968), 325–52.

of fragments from which the spectator must assemble the complete picture. What we get from them depends upon our ability to fill in the missing connectives. The point can be illustrated by looking at a short poem by Guillaume Apollinaire:

> Three lit gas jets
> The proprietor has lung trouble
> When you've finished we'll have a game of backgammon
> A conductor who has a sore throat
> When you come to Tunis I'll have you smoke some kiff
>
> It seems to rhyme.[12]

These lines may evoke the experience of sitting in a Parisian café, but all of the elements are independent, existing side by side. The sequence is unimportant, the connectives are missing.

Much the same quality is found in Antonin Artaud's *Jet of Blood*, a Surrealist play written in 1925. Here is a typical passage:

> *Night suddenly falls. Earthquake. Thunder shakes the air, and lightning zigzags in all directions. In the intermittent flashes of lightning one sees people running around in panic, embracing each other, falling down, getting up again, and running around like madmen. At a given moment an enormous hand seizes the Whore's hair, which bursts into ever-widening flames.*
> A THUNDEROUS VOICE: Bitch, look at your body.
> *The Whore's body appears completely nude under her dress, which suddenly becomes transparent.*

[12] Guillaume Apollinaire, "Lundi Rue Christine," quoted *ibid.*, 333.

THE WHORE: Leave me, God.

She bites God's wrist. An immense jet of blood shoots across the stage, and we can see The Priest making the sign of the cross during a flash of lightning that lasts longer than the others. When the lights come up again, all the characters are dead and their bodies lie scattered over the ground. Only the Young Man and the Whore are left. They are eating each other's eyes.[13]

This segment is taken from the middle of a very short play composed almost entirely of similar fleeting and violent images. Each segment is set off from the others; thus it is up to the reader to deduce how they are connected.

Jet of Blood illustrates, perhaps in an extreme way, those qualities most often criticized in modern art: abruptness, illogicality, obscurity. Before the modern period, this play would have been considered unfinished, inept, unacceptable. In fact, much that is praised in modern times would have been considered pure amateurishness in earlier periods. Artaud, however, is not trying here to capture that sense of rational order that earlier ages thought essential. Rather, he sees reality as a series of fleeting images dredged up from the subconscious mind. Since it differs from logical thought, it must

[13] Antonin Artaud, *Jet of Blood*, trans. George E. Wellwarth, in *Modern French Theatre: The Avant-Garde, Dada, and Surrealism*, an anthology of plays edited and translated by Michael Benedikt and George E. Wellwarth (New York, 1966), 221–26. The passage quoted here is from p. 225.

be conveyed by different, seemingly illogical means.

The Absurdists were the inheritors of the structure used by Maeterlinck and the Surrealists. Their outlook differed somewhat from that of their predecessors, but the structural results were not significantly different. Since they see the world as irrational, they, like Maeterlinck, provide a sequence of events without showing the causal relationships among them. Thus, in Beckett's *Waiting for Godot*, one event follows another but the order is relatively unimportant. Taken all together, they are significant because they imply that man waits and hopes but that his hopes remain unfulfilled. Thus the activities in which the characters participate are primarily ways of passing the time.

The Happening, a form that caught the public fancy in the late 1950s and early 1960s, is a logical extension of what had already been done by the Symbolists, Surrealists, and Absurdists.[14] The earlier movements had implied that reality is made up of juxtaposed occurrences, the significance of which the spectator must deduce as best he can. The Happening merely carried this implication a step further by suggesting that the most truthful art is that which is made up of random occurrences within a loosely controlled framework. One of

[14] For discussions of Happenings, see Michael Kirby (ed.), *Happenings* (New York, 1966); and Richard Kostelanetz, *The Theatre of Mixed Means: An Introduction to Happenings, Kinetic Environments, and Other Mixed-Means Performances* (New York, 1968).

the most influential figures in this movement was John Cage, who created a considerable sensation in the 1950s with his musical composition, *4'33"*. It consisted of a pianist's coming onto the stage, sitting at the piano, and doing nothing for four minutes and thirty-three seconds. Cage declared that the composition was made up of all the random sounds that occurred during that period anywhere within hearing of those in the auditorium.

Cage defines theatre as "things to see and things to hear." Thus, to him the purpose of theatre is to make people more aware of life around them. He declares that we should forget about judging and ranking works and about an artist's intentions. Rather, each person should get out of an art work whatever he can. He states, "I am interested in non-intention, and I think that life is essentially non-intentional." He labels any art that tries to impose a particular response on an audience "police work," since it forces people to respond in a particular way.[15]

But most practitioners of Happenings were more prescriptive than was Cage and most provided a greater amount of structure for their works than did he. Often there were rather elaborate preparations of a place, of special lighting, properties, and seating. Those who attended were typically given slips of paper telling them where to sit or what to do at specific moments. Usually these slips were passed out at random—that is, no one knew in advance who would get which set of directions.

[15] These ideas are expressed in an interview with John Cage in Kostelanetz, *The Theatre of Mixed Means*, 51–63.

Often a number of things were going on simultaneously. The work ended when all the tasks had been completed.[16] In the Happening, the boundaries between life and art were broken down. Usually the audience and the performers were the same, for those who attended were the participants in the activities. Each person experienced the work as he would life itself—that is, he became a participant in events rather than a mere spectator —and from what he himself did and from what he experienced of the things going on around him, he deduced whatever he could. The emphasis was upon the process rather than upon a completed product. There was no intention of creating a script that could be written down in a book or a painting that could be hung on a museum wall. The artwork, like the life process, became unrepeatable. The interest in Happenings declined rapidly during the 1960s, perhaps because they were so uncontrolled that they ultimately were unsatisfying. They provided novelty but little enlightenment and few new insights.

As this brief survey suggests, there are two main uses to which the organization around theme or thought has been put: to suggest the irrationality of the world, and to provide a demonstration or argument. Both are evident in today's theatre, and in the most characteristic drama are merged.

---

[16] For a description of various types of Happenings, see Introduction, Kirby (ed.), *Happenings*, 9–42. The remainder of this book is devoted to outlines of Happenings by various artists or groups.

In an earlier essay I have argued that many contemporary dramatists accept Sartre's notion that ours is
essentially an irrational universe but that nevertheless
each person must find some set of values upon which he
can take a stand and that he must act consistently within
that framework. Since the 1960s, as commitment to specific positions on social, political, moral, and personal issues has increased, dramatists have taken up positions as
well. Although they probably do not consider the world
any more rational than did the Absurdists, they do not
refuse to act. Rather, they have tried to move beyond
absurdity by declaring that, if there is no supernatural
power ruling over the universe, man is even more than
in the past compelled to bring order out of the irrationality and create a framework within which life may
be made as meaningful as possible. Thus, even if a decision is illogical, it is better to act than merely to wait.

In writing committed plays, dramatists have taken
many clues from Brecht. As indicated earlier, one of the
characteristic types of contemporary drama is the parable, which indirectly argues for a particular point of
view or line of action. Most contemporary dramatists,
however, borrow as much from Artaud, Happenings, and
other sources as they do from Brecht.

A good example of recent drama which synthesizes
many earlier practices is Jean-Claude van Itallie's play
The Serpent,[17] recently performed in New York. When

[17] Jean-Claude van Itallie, *The Serpent: A Ceremony* (New
York, 1969).

the audience enters, the actors are warming up in all parts of the theatre and on the stage. They continue until time for the performance to begin. Then comes a procession, which is accompanied by a kind of percussion music beaten out rhythmically by the actors on their own bodies. Occasionally they freeze and prefigure things that will come later in the play. This procession dissolves into an autopsy, followed by a pantomime intended to recall the assassinations of John Kennedy and Martin Luther King. Then the scene becomes the Garden of Eden, and the temptation, fall, and expulsion of Adam and Eve are enacted. This is followed by a series of statements, many of them highly personal, others philosophic. Then comes the Cain and Abel story, followed by "Blind Man's Hell," during which the actors grope their way about the stage, and continuing through a second group of statements. Next comes a reading of a lengthy passage from Genesis (which enumerates the various generations who came after Adam), accompanied by pantomimes of meetings among couples, matings, births, child-rearing, and so on. Eventually everyone grows old and lines up across the front of the stage. The play ends with this stage direction: "The actors move about freely on the stage. Each is overtaken by a slow kind of dying, not so much a physical one as a kind of 'emptying out,' a living death which soon slows them to a complete stop. Each actor has a final small physical tremor. Then, as if ghosts, the actors begin to sing a sentimental popular song from twenty or thirty years ago.

No longer as ghosts but as themselves they continue singing the song as they leave the theatre, walking out through the audience."

This play exhibits many features typical of much, though by no means all, contemporary drama. First, the action is discontinuous—that is, apparently unconnected events are juxtaposed. Second, time and place are completely fluid, since scenes from widely varying times and places are mingled. Third, there is almost no concern for scenery, and the actors improvise what they need as they go along. This is true of sound effects as well. Fourth, the actors shift identities rapidly, the same performer playing many different parts and even, at times, himself. Furthermore, there is little concern for individualizing the characters. Adam and Eve are treated as ritualized figures, rather than as personalities. The players speak the lines and perform the actions of characters, but there is no pretense that they are the characters they present. No actor changes costume at any time; all wear a kind of neutral uniform throughout. Thus, the emphasis is upon significant experiences of mankind rather than upon the story of individuals. Fifth, the play is a parable held together by didactic intentions. It does not impart a lesson directly but uses familiar events (the assassinations of John Kennedy and Martin Luther King) and Biblical material to suggest certain conclusions. Nevertheless, the spectator must deduce the meaning from clues. The basic idea is that the Serpent is something within man that makes him break the limits set on him, whereas God is an idea that man has invented in order to set limits on himself. Thus, God equals conformity, the Serpent freedom. The Kennedy-King and Cain-Abel material suggests that since our contemporary limitations have led to so much violence, we need to make new choices which will lead us out of the present morass. The play is more complex than I have suggested, but these are its basic messages. This need to seek meanings illustrates another characteristic of much contemporary drama—that is, what on the surface seems illogical often turns out to be near-allegorical.

Although *The Serpent* is representative of much contemporary drama, it is more obscure than many didactic plays, which are often all too clear. Perhaps the most extreme instances are found in guerrilla theatre. For example, Marc Estrin suggests a piece called "The Military Execution of the Bill of Rights," as a way of dramatizing repressions. At a public meeting, an unannounced group of performers dressed as soldiers march in and set up a stake to which is pinned the Bill of Rights. As each article is read, the soldiers fire machine guns to execute it. Of this piece, Estrin writes, "This . . . is a simple, effective way of getting attention when beginning a rally, and of announcing its major theme in a way which will attract the media . . . the point being to get the message into sixty million homes." [18] Guerrilla theatre often resembles a Happening given a political turn.

[18] Marc Estrin, "An American Playground Sampler," in William M. Hoffman (ed.), *New American Plays* (3 vols.; New York, 1970), III, 223–39. The piece discussed here is found on pp. 228–29.

A few writers, primarily Peter Weiss, Heinar Kippardt, and Rolf Hochhuth, have turned to documentary drama as a didactic medium. They take official records and other materials relating to actual events and persons and from them shape dramas. In this way, plays have been written about the Auschwitz concentration camp, about the Senate hearings into the loyalty of J. Robert Oppenheimer, about Pope Pius' role in the extermination of the German Jews, and other subjects.[19] Although the authors usually profess objectivity, they almost always shape the evidence, through selection and arrangement, to support a particular point of view. Nevertheless, their arguments carry considerable weight because the audience knows that the events and persons are historically real.

A few writers—such as Arthur Miller and Neil Simon —are still working along traditional lines, but their numbers seem to lessen each year. More and more, we appear to have entered an age of idea-centered drama in which the cause-to-effect arrangement has steadily declined in favor with writers. It seems probable, however, that the majority of spectators still prefer traditional structural patterns. Thought-centered drama, by nature diffuse, all too often fails to provide enough clues to identify the idea used to unify a play. In these cases, the

[19] The works referred to here are Peter Weiss, *The Investigation*, English version by Jon Swan and Ulu Grosbard (New York, 1966) ; Heinar Kippardt, *In the Matter of J. Robert Oppenheimer*, trans. Ruth Spiers (New York, 1968) ; and Rolf Hochhuth, *The Deputy*, trans. Richard and Clara Winston (New York, 1964) .

uninitiated spectator can well find himself lost in a guessing game, one that he frequently decides is not worth the trouble. As a result, the intention of much contemporary drama is misunderstood because its structure (in which disparate elements are juxtaposed thematically) still seems novel, even impenetrable. But if audiences were to cease demanding the logic of cause-and-effect and be content with a series of related impressions, they would find that contemporary drama can provide pleasures as intense as those aroused by traditional works.

FOUR / The Problem of Communication: Brain or Viscera?

C‌ONFLICTS in values and novel structural patterns both contribute to misconceptions about contemporary theatre. Both are also involved in still another significant issue: the means to be used in communicating with the spectator. Should one appeal to his brain or his viscera? Is man essentially a reflecting or a reflexive creature? These questions are crucial, for how we conceive of man ultimately influences our decisions about the techniques most capable of affecting theatre audiences.

Such an inquiry is not applicable to the theatre alone, for today it is even more urgent in the world at large. No one needs to be reminded that many persons now believe that logical argumentation has proven bankrupt —that its user is commended for his rationality, nonviolence, and peaceableness, but that his listeners then merely go on with whatever they were doing before. In other words, it is considered ineffective and an excuse for not acting. What, then, is recommended as an alternative? Something that will jar people out of their comfortable ruts—demonstrations, violence or threats of violence, the burning or bombing of buildings. The usual argument is that when rational means go unheeded, irrational ones become the only possibility. Implicit in this position is the belief that the brain can be reached only after some more elemental response has been aroused—that though the brain is a faculty of understanding, alone it is too disinterested and unfeeling to initiate action. To be effective, then, argument must be made personal—it must somehow lead the hearer to feel involved rather than detached, perhaps through fear or anger make him wish to act. Also implicit in this argument is the conclusion that to comprehend is not enough—that understanding without action is useless.

Nowhere are the current divisions in our society more evident than in conflicting opinions about appropriate ways of expressing dissent and urging action. One cannot live in the United States today without having some familiarity with the techniques used to encourage the adoption of specific points of view or lines of action about political, social, economic, or moral problems. Many of these devices have found their way into the theatre, although some have been modified in the process.

The techniques now in use are, of course, not entirely new. It has always been taken for granted that the theatre should affect an audience emotionally. From classical to modern times the basic purposes of the theatre were said to be to teach and to please. It was also commonly assumed that pleasure was secondary to teaching, that entertainment merely made learning more acceptable. In this theory, it is the head that is ultimately addressed but by way of the senses. It was assumed that once the medicine had been absorbed it would be rationally comprehended and result in moral action. As Sir Philip Sidney wrote in the sixteenth century, "The . . . end of all earthly learning [is] virtuous action." [1]

Until the end of the eighteenth century, tragedy was said to depict the terrible results of wandering from the paths of righteousness, and comedy, treating as it does more mundane subjects, to show how men become ridiculous through foibles. Thus, tragedy was thought to make the spectator fearful of falling into mortal sin, and comedy to make him wary of appearing ridiculous in the eyes of his fellow men. In both cases, it was assumed that the audience, after seeing deviant behavior punished and virtue rewarded, would apply the lessons to their own lives. The appeals were emotional, made by establishing bonds of sympathy or antipathy between spectator and characters, but the ultimate application was rational. The basic aims, therefore, probably did not differ, except in the way they were stated, from those now being advocated. The specific kinds of response expected from the audience did differ, however, as did the means used to reach the audience. In those earlier years, the means were primarily the characters' speeches, in which their moral bents, motivations, and decisions were clearly set forth; the dramatic action developed conflicts between virtuous or depraved agents, normally ending with the triumph of virtue. A cause-to-effect arrangement of incidents was used because it was taken for

[1] Sir Philip Sidney, "The Defense of Poesie," in Allan H. Gilbert (ed.), *Literary Criticism, Plato to Dryden* (New York, 1940), 418.

granted that this is a rational world ruled over by a just god, and that the audience itself is capable of acting rationally. Attention and sympathy were engaged through emotional appeals, but these were ultimately intended to lead to moral perceptions which would then be applied in daily conduct.[2]

The invariable triumph of justice in drama eventually palled, however, perhaps because men came to feel less certain that this is a just world. The many stresses of the eighteenth century that led to the American and French revolutions also, no doubt, contributed to a reexamination of earlier views. For whatever reason, at the end of the eighteenth century the Romantics began to emphasize man's divided nature: the flesh versus the spirit. They depicted man as a creature divided against himself, born with an innate desire for perfection, but denied the achievement of perfection in life by the pressures of material existence. Thus, despite his longings for perfection, man is always thwarted. But the innate impulse toward perfection was considered evidence that there is a supernatural realm, in which perfection is possible. In other words, longings for perfection cannot be fulfilled during earthly existence, but, because man is also a part of the world of eternity, his perfection consists in cultivating the spirit, which can flower fully only after material being is shuffled off.[3]

[2] The Neoclassical vision is covered thoroughly by René Wellek, *A History of Modern Criticism* (4 vols.; New Haven, Conn., 1955), I.

[3] The Romantic period is covered equally thoroughly by Wellek, *A History of Modern Criticism*, II.

Drama came to be seen as a compound of man's material and spiritual impulses, reflecting his desires for perfection even while showing him held back by the temptations and shortcomings of material reality. Philosophers began to argue that the aesthetic experience is uniquely capable of giving man a glimpse into spiritual freedom, for in its grip he is momentarily released from that multitude of conflicting demands made upon him by daily life. Friedrich Schiller saw the aesthetic experience as the only one in which the material and spiritual impulses are united: "All other forms of perception divide the man, because they are based exclusively either in the sensuous or in the spiritual part of his being. It is only the perception of beauty that makes of him an entirety, because it demands the cooperation of his two natures." [4] Somewhat similarly, the German philosopher Immanuel Kant defined art as "disinterested contemplation." [5] In either case, drama, as a form of art, is considered capable of lifting the spectator to a higher plane where he achieves something like a god's-eye view of existence. Momentarily freed from material restrictions, he can contemplate the human condition disinterestedly.

These views probably found their fullest expression in the work of Richard Wagner, who with his music-dramas sought to provide a mystical vision of human destiny capable of lifting audiences out of their mun-

[4] Friedrich Schiller, *On the Aesthetic Education of Man*, ed. and trans. E. M. Wilkinson and L. A. Willoughby (Oxford, 1967), 215.
[5] Immanuel Kant, *Critique of Judgment*, trans. J. H. Bernard (New York, 1951), 45.

dane existence. He argues that the dramatist is a myth-maker rather than a retailer of domestic intrigues. For him, the ideal work consists of a Teutonic myth (or mythlike story) embodied in a union of drama and music, something like a synthesis of Shakespeare and Beethoven, in which drama is "dipped in the magic fountain of music" to create and preserve ideality. The ultimate purpose is to unify and give meaning to a whole culture through a communal experience which lifts the audience to an idealized plane of being.[6]

Having set himself the task of creating such works, Wagner went on to suggest appropriate means. First, he demanded a new kind of theatre, which he eventually attained in the Bayreuth Festspielhaus, designed especially for his works. It included architectural elements—two proscenium arches and a sunken orchestra pit—intended to mark a clear division—what Wagner called the "mystic chasm"—between the ideal world (the stage) and the real world (the auditorium). Wagner wished to draw the audience across this chasm and thus transport it into the ideal world of the drama. To accomplish this, he considered an absolute illusion necessary. Consequently, he hid the orchestra from the audience's view, refused to permit the musicians to tune up in the pit, forbade applause during performances, would not let

[6] Richard Wagner's ideas on the theatre are scattered throughout his works. Many of the most important are developed in *Opera and Drama*, trans. Edwin Evans (London, 1913). Selections from *The Purpose of Drama* are included in *European Theories of the Drama*, edited by Barrett H. Clark and revised by Henry Popkin (New York, 1965), 289–96.

the actors take curtain calls, and organized his works so that there were no set arias or showpieces like those in traditional opera. His conception of illusion is summed up in one of his statements about the hidden orchestra: "I next should lay especial stress on the invisibility of the orchestra." Because in traditional theatres the conductor and the orchestra are seen, the spectator "is made an unwilling witness to technical evolutions which should be almost as carefully concealed from him as the cords, ropes, laths, and scaffoldings of the stage decoration —which, seen from the wings, as everyone knows, destroy all vestige of illusion." [7]

In addition to concealing the mechanism by which illusion is created, Wagner also insisted that every element of production—the music, the drama, the directing, the scenery, the acting, the costumes, the lighting— should either be created or closely supervised by the same person so that all are conceived as a single unit. He also thought that each element should underscore the dramatic values in each scene and in the play as a whole. Thus, Wagner set forth the ideal of unified production in much the way it was to be accepted in the modern theatre.

Wagner's ultimate concern, however, was the audience's experience. He sought to arouse in the spectator an irresistible empathic response. He wished to overpower the audience, pull it across the "mystic chasm," and force it to participate in the idealized experience (or "master art work," as he called it). In this notion

[7] Richard Wagner, *Prose Works*, trans. William Ashton Ellis (8 vols.; New York, 1966), III, 276–77.

lies one of Wagner's principal influences on the modern theatre—the belief that the success of a production is determined by its ability to engage the audience's emotions and to draw the spectator into the world of the play.

Wagner's goal of creating an idealized drama was certainly not shared by all his contemporaries in the late nineteenth century. On the contrary, many of them championed Realistic or Naturalistic works designed to focus attention upon the real, rather than the ideal, world.[8] They considered Wagner's dramas escapist. But, though they did not agree with his ultimate aims, they, for the most part, accepted his notion about means. They too sought to hide the theatre's mechanisms, to create a complete illusion of reality, and to evoke an empathic response. They too came to subscribe to the theory that unity of production is essential and that all theatrical elements should underscore the dramatic values of each scene.

Wagner's ideas were picked up by Adolphe Appia and Gordon Craig and through their versions came to dominate modern theatrical theory.[9] Thus, Wagner must be

[8] The major spokesman for Naturalism was Émile Zola, especially in *Le Naturalisme au théâtre* (Paris, 1881). Few of his writings on the theatre have been translated into English. One selection, however, is readily available: "Preface to *Thérèse Raquin*," in Clark (ed.), *European Theories of the Drama*, 377–79. Zola's theories are treated at length in Lawson A. Carter, *Zola and the Theatre* (New Haven, Conn., 1963).

[9] Adolphe Appia's major works are *Music and the Art of the Theatre*, trans. Robert W. Corrigan and Mary Douglas Dirks (Coral Gables, Fla., 1962), and *The Work of Living Art*, trans. H. D. Albright (Coral Gables, 1960). Gordon Craig's major works are *On the Art of the Theatre* (London, 1911), and *The Theatre Advancing* (Boston, 1919).

considered one of the principal influences upon the twentieth-century stage. But Wagner's views did not go unchallenged. One might point to many theorists who disagreed with him, but the most significant today is Bertolt Brecht.[10] In fact, many of Brecht's ideas seem motivated by a desire to refute Wagner's conception of the theatrical experience.

Brecht begins with the assumption that the kind of hypnotic effect sought by Wagner is fundamentally wrong, since it reduces the audience to a completely passive role. In Wagner's theatre, the spectator is acted upon—he is expected to contribute only his willingness to be absorbed into the play's illusion. Perhaps the ultimate purpose is to make of him a better human being by providing him an idealized experience, but only indirectly, if at all, is he expected to translate the theatrical experience into practical action outside the theatre.

Brecht wished to redefine this relationship among spectator, theatre, and society, and consequently had to employ novel devices. To make it clear that he sought a new effect, Brecht called his approach "epic" to distinguish it from the "dramatic" theatre, against which he was in revolt. He declared that the dramatic theatre has outlived its usefulness because it has reduced the spectator to complete passivity; in it, social conditions appear to be fixed and unchangeable, for, even if historical subjects are treated, they are presented in modern terms and thus give the impression that things have

[10] See Chap. 3, footnote 8.

always been as they now are. Furthermore, illusionistic staging gives everything such an air of stability that traditional values are made to appear entrenched and permanent. Since everything seems fixed, the spectator can only watch, for nothing else is left for him to do.

Instead of this traditional theatre, Brecht envisioned a new one in which the audience would play a vital and active role. He insisted that the spectator should watch performances critically. While the theatre should be entertaining, it brings its "greatest pleasure" through "productive participation," in which the spectator actively judges and applies what he sees on the stage to conditions outside the theatre. But if the spectator is to watch in this active way, he must be assisted in playing his part. Hence, Brecht adopted a whole set of techniques which differed markedly from those used by Wagner.

Perhaps the most important term in Brecht's theory is *alienation,* or more literally, the process of "making strange," of distancing the spectator from the events so that he can watch critically. Whereas Wagner wanted a total empathic response, Brecht sought to short-circuit empathy by breaking the illusion and reminding the audience that it is in a theatre watching a reflection of reality, not reality itself—that the real problems lie outside the theatre, not on the stage. To jar the audience out of its empathic responses, Brecht used a number of technical devices. These include songs, narrative passages, filmed sequences, projected captions or pictures, direct address to the audience, and many others.

Unlike Wagner, who sought to hide the mechanism

of the theatre, Brecht revealed it. He mounted lighting instruments where they would be visible, changed scenery in full view of the audience, and placed musicians onstage with the actors. Instead of full-stage, realistic settings, he used fragmentary scenery or projections. To him, scenery should serve only to locate the action or to comment on it; it should not seek to give the illusion of a place in its entirety. Not only did he in this way seek to avoid illusionism, he also sought to discourage any sense of permanence or unchangeability. His approach is perhaps summed up in this verse:

> . . . let the spectator
> Be aware of busy preparations, made for him
> Cunningly; he sees a tinfoil moon
> Float down, or a tiled roof
> Being carried in; do not show him too much,
> But show him something.[11]

Brecht advised his actors not to impersonate a character so much as to *present* the behavior of a particular kind of person in a particular type of situation. He declared his opposition to Konstantin Stanislavsky's system of acting, and told his performers that, rather than trying to live their roles, they should stand outside and comment upon them. This approach was extended to all the other elements of production as well. In this idea can be seen another difference between Brecht and Wagner. Brecht rejected Wagner's conception of uni-

[11] Bertolt Brecht, "Die Vorhaenge," in Siegfried Unseld (ed.), *Schriften zum Theater* (Frankfurt, 1957), 260.

fied production, calling it redundant, since music, scenery, lighting, costumes, and acting all seek to convey the same qualities. On the other hand, Brecht wanted each element to comment in a different way. For example, he declared that in a satirical song the music need not be satirical, since the words or acting would convey satire, but might preferably contradict expectations. This juxtaposition of two contrary moods would then create conflict in the mind of the spectator, forcing him to reconcile the two elements. Thus the spectator is forced to think instead of merely being lulled by the music. Similarly, a costume may be composed of several disparate elements. While it should give some information about place and time, it should also comment on the character and the issues.

Ultimately, the differences between Brecht and Wagner are attributable to their conceptions of how the audience should respond. Wagner wished to transport the spectators out of their world; Brecht wanted to make them more critically aware of their society. Wagner sought to create a compelling illusion; Brecht sought to interrupt illusion and keep the audience aware that it is in a theatre. In Wagner's terms, Brecht insists that the audience look at the stage from the wings—that is, with all the machinery showing. Brecht adopted this method so that he might emphasize the difference between contemplating fictional problems and real ones. Thus, according to Brecht the theatre should not be an escape from reality but an inducement to cope with reality more meaningfully. Wagner was a sensualist—that is, he wanted to appeal so powerfully to the senses that the spectator would give himself up to the experience. Brecht was an intellectual, for, although he did not deny the power of the senses, he treated them as merely preliminary to thought.

In recent years, Wagner's influence has declined considerably while Brecht's has steadily increased. Perhaps the most influential aspect of Brecht's thought has been the notion that the theatre should serve as an instrument for change in society. Several of his techniques have also been adopted, but to many contemporary practitioners his devices seem inadequate. This dissatisfaction is probably explained by changed conceptions of the audience. Brecht always proceeds on the assumption that man is capable of reflecting and of reaching wise decisions, if he is provided the proper demonstrations. But if one comes to believe that rational appeals are ineffective, that man acts only when he feels threatened, then Brecht's devices are perhaps too mild, too conservative. Consequently, many theatre workers have looked elsewhere for guidance.

Since World War II, the most influential theorist has been Antonin Artaud, author of *The Theatre and Its Double,* published in 1938.[12] According to Artaud, the theatre in the Western world has been devoted to a

12 Antonin Artaud, *The Theatre and Its Double* was translated into English by Mary Caroline Richards and published in New York in 1958. The most authoritative edition of Artaud's writings is *Oeuvres* (7 vols.; Paris, 1956–67). Although I have worked from the French text, I refer here when possible to the English translations.

very narrow range of human experience, primarily the psychological problems of individuals or the social problems of groups (in other words, experiences related to what Freud calls the conscious mind). To Artaud, on the other hand, the most important aspects of existence are submerged in the unconscious mind.

Artaud calls the Western world's use of the theatre mistaken. He declares that in the West the theatre has been looked upon as a preserver of culture, something like a museum, rather than as a living experience. For this reason, he says, the theatre has become the property of an elite group and has been cut off from the masses. But Artaud declares: "I consider that the world is hungry and that it doesn't care about culture. . . . The most urgent thing is not so much to defend a culture whose existence never saved a man from the worry of living or of being hungry, as to extract from what we call culture some ideas whose living force is identical to hunger." [13] Artaud considers all those things that we call "civilization" to be a numbing overlay of a deeper, more elemental culture. He argues that our form of civilization will eventually fall into oblivion "and the spaceless, timeless culture which is contained in our nervous capacities will reappear with an increased energy." [14] To help us reach that better state, we need a theatre that stirs up feeling rather than ideas.

Artaud clearly differs from both Wagner and Brecht in his views of human needs. Wagner seems to believe

[13] Artaud, *The Theatre and Its Double*, 7.
[14] *Ibid.*, 10.

that man is missing some higher spiritual vision, and Brecht that man needs an incentive to forge a new society. But Artaud sees man's problems as those buried in the subterranean reaches of the mind, those things that cause divisions within man and between men, those things that lead to hatred, violence, and disaster. For Artaud, then, the theatre should serve a near-psychiatric function, but for the whole society and not merely the individual. The goal is something like a religious experience in which a true communion—the elimination of all divisions—is reached.

The theatre that Artaud envisions is akin to ritual, and its basic subject matter is mythic. But his view of myth is quite unlike that of Wagner, who tended to see it as uplifting and idealized. Artaud, on the contrary, states, "The great myths are dark, so that one cannot imagine, save in an atmosphere of carnage, torture, and bloodshed, all the magnificent fables which recount to the multitudes the first sexual division and the first carnage . . . in creation." [15] Artaud also states that we cannot return to the myths of the past—such as those of the Greeks and Christians—for these have lost their power to affect us sufficiently. Rather, new myths will arise out of something like a plague which destroys repressive social forms. "Order collapses, authority evaporates, anarchy prevails and man gives vent to all the disordered impulses which lie buried in his soul." [16] It should be emphasized, however, that Artaud sees all these things occurring *in* the

[15] *Ibid.*, 31.
[16] *Ibid.*, 16.

theatre rather than outside it, for his theatre is to serve the function of cleansing society. According to Artaud, man, if given the proper theatrical experiences, can be freed from ferocity and can then express the joy which civilization has forced him to repress. The theatre will evacuate those feelings which are usually expressed in more destructive ways. "I defy that spectator to give himself up, once outside the theatre, to ideas of war, riot, and blatant murder." [17] The theatre, "impelling men to see themselves as they are, causes the mask to fall, reveals the lie, the slackness, baseness, and hypocrisy of the world." [18] Or, as Artaud puts it most succinctly, "the theatre has been created to drain abcesses collectively." [19]

It is clear that Artaud considers the world sick—a madman needing shock treatments. The theatre is to be the instrument of healing. And the cure is to consist of removing all those things which divide men. The goal is complete harmony. But how is this to be achieved? Artaud is certain that it cannot be done through appeals to the rational mind. Rather, it will be necessary to operate directly upon the senses, for the conscious mind has been conditioned to sublimate the most fundamental human impulses. Thus, it is necessary to break down the audience's defenses.

Artaud sometimes refers to his as a Theatre of Cruelty, since in order to achieve its ends it must force the audience to confront itself. He declares that the theatre re-

[17] *Ibid.*, 82.
[18] *Ibid.*, 31.
[19] *Ibid.*

quires a force similar to a plague if it is to be effective. "In the theatre as in the plague there is something both triumphant and vengeful." [20] But the cruelty Artaud advocates is not primarily physical, but moral: "We are not talking about that cruelty which we can exert on one another by cutting up each other's bodies, by sawing on our personal anatomies." [21] Rather, it is an extramoral identification which will take hold of us physically, kinesthetically. About his production of *The Cenci*, Artaud explains that it is not a question of "purely corporal cruelty but a moral one; it goes to the extremity of instinct and forces the actor to plunge right to the roots of his being so that he leaves the stage exhausted. A cruelty which acts as well upon the spectator and should not allow him to leave the theatre intact, but exhausted, involved, perhaps transformed." [22]

To achieve this transformation, he seeks what he calls a new language of the theatre. Much impressed by Oriental art with its symbolic, ritualized elements, he argues that the Western theatre can be reformed only by the use of comparable means, although he recognizes that Eastern devices cannot be taken over directly.

Part of his interest in the Eastern theatre stems from his discontent with the West's emphasis on language and the consequent appeal to the rational mind. As he puts it: "Whereas most people remain impervious to a subtle discourse whose intellectual development escapes them,

[20] *Ibid.*, 27.
[21] Artaud, *Oeuvres*, IV, 95.
[22] *Ibid.*, V, 309.

they cannot resist effects of physical surprise, the dynamism of cries and violent movements, visual explosions, the aggregate of tetanizing effects called up on cue and used to act in a direct manner on the physical sensitivity of the spectators. Carried along by the paroxysms of a violent physical action which no sensitivity can resist, the spectator finds his over-all nervous system becoming sharpened and refined." [23] Artaud's intention of operating directly on the nervous system, of evoking a kinesthetic response, leads him to suggest many new devices for the theatre.

Among these is the abandonment of the traditional theatre building. To replace it, he suggests remodeled barns, factories, or airplane hangars. He wishes to locate acting areas in corners, on overhead catwalks, along the walls. Spectators will be furnished with swivel chairs that will permit them to turn in any direction. They will be surrounded by the action. Artaud states: "There will be no decor. That will be adequately taken care of by hieroglyphic actors, ritualistic costumes, puppets thirty feet tall representing King Lear's beard in the storm, musical instruments as tall as a man, objects of unheard of form and purpose." [24]

In lighting, he advocates a "vibrating, shredded" effect. He calls for "flashes of light whose nature changes, goes from red to a crude pink, from silver to green, then turns white, with suddenly an immense opaque yellow

[23] *Ibid.*, II, 187.
[24] Artaud, *The Theatre and Its Double*, 97–98.

light the color of dirty fog and dust storms." [25] He adds that each "hue will be as complex and subtle as anguish." [26] Sound is treated in much the same way. He favors shrillness, staccato effects, and abrupt changes in volume. In his script for *The Cenci,* he suggests that a scene set in a torture chamber should "give off the noise of a factory at peak production." [27] When he staged the play, he used a screeching wheel which produced an almost intolerable sound. He also employed an electronic device that could vary volume from the softest tones to those louder than a full symphony orchestra. There was also a great deal of vocal, nonverbal sound, for he used the human voice not so much as an instrument of discursive speech as of tonalities, prolonged modulations, yelps, barks, as a creator of harmony or dissonance. About language, he says: "Why is it that in the theatre, at least theatre as we know it in . . . the West, everything that is specifically theatrical, namely everything that . . . is not contained in dialogue . . . is left in the background? I say that the stage is a physical and concrete place that demands to be filled, and demands that one make it speak its own concrete language." This language should be "addressed first of all to the senses rather than to the mind, as is the case with the language of words," because "the public thinks first of all with its senses." [28]

Both Brecht and Artaud wrote most of their major

[25] Artaud, *Oeuvres,* II, 91.
[26] *Ibid.*
[27] *Ibid.,* IV, 263.
[28] Artaud, *The Theatre and Its Double,* 37, 38, 85.

works before World War II but their influence was not strongly felt until later. Today, Artaud's influence on theatrical means seems greater than Brecht's, while on goals Brecht's influence seems greater than Artaud's. Actually, their ideas have been mingled and altered rather freely so that today's theatre is neither Brechtian nor Artaudian, but a synthesis of the two.

Clearly the Wagnerian influence is waning. The framed stage and concealed mechanisms no longer seem necessary. The open stage, the arena stage, the utilization of spaces never intended for theatrical use are now common in theatrical production. We no longer believe it necessary to lull an audience into accepting as actual, or nearly actual, the theatrical events transpiring on stage. Consequently, it no longer seems necessary to hide the theatre's means—the lighting instruments, the musicians, the scene changes, and so on. We are willing to accept the theatre *as theatre* rather than pretending that it is a mock-real world.

It is the Broadway theatre that most nearly continues the Wagnerian ideal. All that Wagner asked of his audience was that it give itself up to the experience; he idealistically believed that in this way he could stretch and extend his audiences both emotionally and spiritually. Most Broadway producers do not aim to stretch audiences spiritually, but, like Wagner, they do ask that the audience be nonresisting. If Wagner's idealism is removed, there is left merely the theatre of escape, theatre as a form of recreation.

But serious playwrights and producers see the theatre

as something more than relaxation, and they make demands on the audience in excess of mere passive participation. Brecht wanted the spectator to think, to reach decisions, to leave the theatre and change society. Artaud wanted to assault the audience, to break down its resistance, to purge it morally and spiritually. Unlike Wagner, who sought to transport the audience outside itself, Artaud sought to force the spectator to confront himself and through the process to cleanse himself and find harmony with his fellow man.

Artaud's unwillingness for the audience to be comfortable has been taken over by many contemporary theatre groups. The results are often similar to those found these days in audience-speaker relationships. It used to be assumed that a speaker would be listened to quietly, then perhaps be questioned; usually, whether it agreed or not, the audience went home peacefully without making any public response beyond polite applause. Nowadays a speaker cannot even count on being heard, for such an occasion has been redefined until it is no longer merely a one-way communication. It is now a dialogue, often more nearly a confrontation. An analogous situation, though reversed, has developed in the theatre. The audience used to assume that it would be permitted to go to the theatre, sit quietly, liking or disliking what it saw, not being expected to make any overt response beyond applause. But some theatrical groups no longer consider this sufficient. Some, such as the Living Theatre, have insisted upon direct confrontation with their audiences, shouting at them, spitting on them if they object to anything, in general treating the theatrical experience as a meeting in which conflicting views are to be brought into the open and fought out. This kind of audience-performer situation, fortunately, seems to be on the way out, for, in current jargon, it has proved counterproductive.

Earlier it was stated that some contemporary groups have adopted a Brechtian view of the purpose of theatre —to encourage social action. Few of these companies, however, have accepted that part of Brecht's theory which states that the spectator should make up his own mind. Most are unwilling to let the audience do its own thinking, and instead urge specific lines of action. Some are merely negative. They ridicule or cast doubt on accepted values or practices but make no suggestions about positive alternatives.

Although a great many contemporary playwrights and directors are primarily interested in social problems, others are closer to Artaud in their concern with the psychological and seek to break down the inhibitions upon which social mores depend. Few, however, have Artaud's concern for reaching a communion among all men. Some are merely anarchic—that is, they wish to break down all authority and substitute individual values for it. They seek a society in which every man will merely do "his own thing" without interference.

What all these approaches have in common, however, is a certain view of the audience—of the kind of creature man is. Almost all seem to assume that the audience is alogical, that it must be approached through its senses.

Consequently, many directors place great emphasis on sound, light, movement, pulsating rhythm.[29] Situations tend to be conceived broadly in terms of basic human experiences—ones typical of humanity in general or of groups rather than of private individuals—and the emotional demands tend to be elemental—a worthy cause or group being threatened by unfeeling or cruel forces. Thought is often reduced to the level of the slogan—subtleties are eliminated for the sake of making issues clear-cut. We are asked to feel for the persecuted, to hate the persecutor. Often the villain is a society which represses deviational behavior, which is treated as superior to the false values advocated by the oppressors. Behind most of the plays is a rather romantic vision of man as a creature capable of perfection if he were not dehumanized by a society which forces him into the wrong mold. Thus, the perfection of man requires as a first step that he be freed from false restraints. Most of the plays, however, do not state this view directly but merely imply it. The message is to be absorbed through the nerves, the pores, the muscles. The brain is considered a deceiver which must be subverted by appeals against which it is helpless.

Still, there is considerable ambivalence in all this. As suggested earlier,[30] many of today's plays cannot be fully

[29] The director who has gained most attention with these means is Tom O'Horgan. As for playwrights, it is those associated with the LaMama Experimental Theatre Club who have been most consistently dedicated to new modes.

[30] See Chap. 3, above.

comprehended until the seemingly unrelated elements are assembled around a concept. If the right concept is not found, the play remains vague, unsatisfying. But it is the brain which must discover the right concept and assemble the parts into a whole. Much the same might be said about language. Most contemporary drama has downgraded the word, and in its former dominant position has put movement, sound, light, and other nonverbal devices. Still, there is a point beyond which perceptions cannot go without resorting to conceptual thought, and conceptual thought depends upon language.

Ultimately, these issues involve hierarchy. Which takes precedence in man: intelligence or feeling? In every period, both have been considered essential; it is merely the relative emphasis placed upon each that has varied. Today, the intellect seems to be under attack, for it is considered a faculty which can easily be subverted through rationalizations. Man is viewed as a creature who acts only when his feelings are affected. Thus, many playwrights seek to make the audience feel personally involved, personally threatened. The mind is approached through the viscera.

FIVE / From Detachment to Commitment

OSCAR WILDE once wrote: "The only beautiful things . . . are the things that do not concern us. As long as a thing is useful or necessary to us, or affects us in any way, either for pain or for pleasure . . . it is outside the proper sphere of art. To art's subject matter we should be more or less indifferent." [1] This conception of art as detached experience contrasts sharply with that voiced recently by Luis Valdez, director of El Teatro Campesino: "I sometimes think the best propaganda comes through and is merged with the best art. In the theatre, art is communication and propaganda; but organizing and politics and teaching are nothing but that, communication. So the more artful you are, not arty, artful, the more propagandistic you are." [2]

Here are two contradictory views of art. Wilde obviously sees it as somehow superior to daily existence and as capable of lifting us above the petty concerns of every-

[1] Oscar Wilde, "The Decay of Lying," in *Intentions* (London, 1891), 16–17.

[2] Program for Radical Theatre Festival, San Francisco State College, September, 1968, p. 19.

day life. Valdez, on the other hand, views it as an experience which leads directly back to life by commenting upon and clarifying it. Wilde, through detachment from the humdrum world, wishes to reach a plane on which questions of usefulness, desirability, pain, and pleasure are irrelevant, whereas Valdez seeks to provoke action by directing attention forcefully to the problems of life around us. These diametrically opposed views pinpoint a crucial issue, for how we conceive the purpose of theatre determines the means we will employ and the responses we will attempt to arouse.

In recent years, there has been a marked trend toward viewing the theatre as a weapon through which to win commitment for specific points of view or lines of action. In fact, many objections voiced against today's theatre stem from the experience of being asked to condone or support antipathetic or repugnant behavior or opinions. Often the spectator is not presented with a balanced view, on the basis of which he can reach a decision, but is bombarded with arguments (either stated or implied) for a position already reached by the playwright or director. He may find his own views on sexual mores, obscenity, the war in Vietnam, the American way of life, political issues, race relations, and a variety of other topics under attack. Many spectators come away from the theatre feeling that they have paid to be harangued, insulted, or humiliated. If they decide that they cannot remain at such a performance, they may sometimes, although now less often than formerly, find themselves verbally assaulted with obscenities or with accusations of favoring murder, genocide, racism, or some other unpleasant view. Despite what one may think of such situations, it is clear that the producers themselves believe they are using the theatre properly—unlike Broadway, which they consider perverted because of its devotion to entertainment designed merely to divert the audience and permit it to remain comfortable in its convictions and prejudices.

Such commitment stands in sharp contrast to the situation that prevailed when I was in college. We were convinced that plays advocating specific points of view on social or political problems were inferior works which should be labeled propaganda rather than art. Even George Bernard Shaw was suspect. No doubt, we were made uneasy by plays about social, economic, or political problems which questioned our way of life and felt much more comfortable with those that focused on the psychological or moral dilemmas of individuals with whom we could sympathize but who posed no direct threat to us. Whatever the explanation, that time now seems remote, a more idyllic period when discussions of plays seldom passed beyond polite exchanges of opinion.

Since about 1960, however, playwrights have gradually moved away from treating the problems of individuals and have turned increasingly to issues as they affect groups or society as a whole. While the characters are obviously still individuals, they are now usually chosen because they represent an attitude about an issue; thus, the focus has shifted to the ideas and away from the characters. The old type of play has not completely disappeared. Arthur Miller's drama *The Price* is an excellent example, but when I saw it not long ago I was struck by how much it already seemed a play from the past. And yet, in the 1950s Miller was considered our most socially conscious playwright. But Miller was always concerned primarily with questions of personal integrity, with what happens to individuals when they compromise with principle. Consequently, his work is character-centered and it contrasts sharply with the dominant stream of today, which is issue-centered. Increasingly, the theatre has become a place for dialectic exchanges between opposing points of view in which individual characters are important only insofar as they represent attitudes about the issues themselves.

Because the theatre has turned increasingly to treating the same conflicts which agitate us in life, our attitudes toward it tend to be affected by our positions on the actual issues, a sign that the theatre has become a more direct mirror of life—some people would say a much too direct one—than it was in the preceding decade. The theatre today also reflects society in its methods. Just as we have turned away from polite exchanges to confrontations, so the theatre has abandoned the objective dramatization of problems in favor of partisan solutions or behavioral responses. The stance of disinterested inquiry has been abandoned in favor of wholehearted commitment. Just as the individual without strong convictions has become something of an anachronism, so too it has become increasingly difficult to find plays that seem neutral.

Ours is, of course, not the only society that has been

faced with stresses, nor is this the first time that the theatre has been used as a weapon. In fact, there can be found in classical Greece, the originator of theatre as we know it, many of the same stresses and many of the same arguments over the theatre's purpose as those of the present. Aristophanes, the great comic dramatist of the late fifth century B.C., voiced an extremely partisan point of view and used methods not unlike those of today.

During most of Aristophanes' productive life, Athens was engaged in a protracted war with Sparta, one that continued for twenty-seven years and to Aristophanes seemed to be undermining all the values for which Athens stood. In a number of plays he attacked the war and sought to show its absurdity. In the most famous of these plays, *Lysistrata,* the women decide to use a sex strike as a device to end the war. In our terms, they stage a sit-in, or more accurately, they seize the Acropolis (that is, the city's fortress). At the same time, they announce their intention of boycotting sex until peace is restored. There is in this play, when accurately translated, far more obscenity and many more explicit sexual references than are found in any play seen on the American stage.

But *Lysistrata* is only one of the plays written by Aristophanes to ridicule the war. In others, he depicted the leaders of Athens as self-serving, limited, and ignorant men.[3] Nor was the war his only target, for he also denounced the inadequacies of the Athenian jury system, the irresponsible teachings of the new rhetoricians (who

[3] As in *The Acharnians* and *Peace.*

he thought were leading young people astray), and dangerous trends in the drama itself.[4]

This social protest was made through devices that caricatured representatives of the various points of view; through episodic stories which were kept entertaining by the liberal use of jokes, songs, dances, and music; and through costumes which emphasized sexual attributes. Most of these elements were not original with Aristophanes but were, by his time, traditional in Greek comedy. Nevertheless, he used these inherited devices to support his own highly partisan and deeply committed views about the issues of his day. When we now read the plays, they seem merely amusing comedies, but when they were written they were as topical and as controversial as a play about Vietnam or President Nixon would be today.

Also like many of our playwrights, Aristophanes was rather self-righteous. In his comedies, he frequently states that it is his duty to counsel the citizens of Athens on proper courses of action, especially so since they are subjected to such bad advice and deception by their political leaders. He obviously considered himself a responsible citizen with an unassailable moral position. Furthermore, he saw no conflict between his moral stance and his use of obscenity, overt sex, and opposition to the war and the political leaders of his day. To him, the purpose of drama was to set forth the principles upon which action should be based. For example, in *The Frogs* he debates the rela-

[4] In, respectively, *The Wasps, The Clouds,* and *The Frogs.*

tive merits of Euripides and Aeschylus as tragic play-wrights. He satirizes Euripides for being more concerned with winning arguments than with the validity of his evidence, and for encouraging people to question traditional values. On the other hand, he praises Aeschylus for establishing an ideal toward which men may strive. Herein lies the major difference between Aristophanes and the playwrights of our day. Aristophanes set himself against departures from traditional Athenian values, and in the war, the new rhetoric, and other contemporary experience he saw enemies of the Athenian way of life. No doubt many of our playwrights would take a similar point of view about the American way of life, but if so, most of them do not articulate their respect for a lost ideal so much as their contempt for what they think our society has become. The point, however, is that during Aristophanes' lifetime the stresses were in many ways similar to those of today and that the theatre was used in a similar manner. Nevertheless, the parallels should not be pushed too far, for the two societies differ greatly, as do their art forms. Still, despite our tendency to view Greek drama as detached and remote, it was not so considered by the Greeks themselves. To them, the plays were concerned with vital philosophical, moral, and social issues. That they have proved universal and lasting does not argue against topicality in their own day.

Herein may lie one of the principal differences between our plays and those of the Greeks—that is, in the relationship of the topical to the universal. Almost all plays that achieve fame in their own time have a strong topical interest for the playgoers of that day. Most do not survive the period in which they were written, except as words on paper which now fail to move us. Those that do interest succeeding generations have what (for want of a better term) is called universality—that is, they contain ideas, characters, or stories that continue to be topical because they capture something meaningful to people in widely separated times and places. It is not the specific circumstances so much as the recurring human situations which make the plays endure. *Hamlet* is not universal because we can ever expect to be in Hamlet's specific situation (that is, as a young prince of Denmark) but because we will be faced with many of Hamlet's dilemmas —the demand to take action in the face of conflicting evidence, the sorrow of discovering duplicity in those who ought to love us, the need to right some grievous wrong—these are recurring motifs in human life, no matter what the specific time and place. Each new generation may find in a play something quite different from what its forebears saw, but so long as the drama strikes some strong sympathetic chord, it is likely to survive.

Thus, topicality, or what today is called "relevance," is not synonymous with a concern for immediate issues. In fact, if it does not extend beyond the purely local it probably will not survive the moment. When we read Aristophanes' plays, it is the highly topical references which interest us least. In fact, without the notes supplied by editors these references would be totally incomprehensible to most of us. What attracts us is the satirical treatment of war, sex, political chicanery, and similar topics.

A great many writers today, however, seem interested only in immediate relevance—in the timely and local. Many of the works have severe drawbacks if we view them as artistic creations—that is, as products which will continue to exist and upon which future generations will pass judgment. How much of the current drama will survive the test of time? Probably very little, but then very little from any generation does.

One major difference between the current generation of writers and those of the past, however, is today's widespread contempt for "art." Many of our writers wish to be relevant and care little about creating enduring artworks. Consequently, many of the questions asked in the past about the nature and purposes of art seem to them irrelevant. The experience *now*, the effect *now* is to them the important thing, and to be concerned about art in the traditional sense is elitist, snobbish, and escapist.

It has become increasingly common in recent years to hear museums characterized as cemeteries—places where artworks of the past can be viewed by those who are more concerned about the dead past than with the living present. The museum, of course, makes a better example than does the theatre, since paintings are fixed, unchanging, and, in one sense, lifeless objects hanging inertly on walls. But this analogy can be extended to the theatre, for its detractors characterize it as an activity which has come to appeal primarily to the affluent middle classes, who go to see works that allow them to remain complacently convinced of their own superiority. The theatre is also said to be run in such a way as to intimidate the uninitiated and its prices to restrict clientele to the affluent. For these and other reasons, the theatre is said to have abdicated its role as a vital force in society and to have become a mere purveyor of escapist entertainment. Many contemporary groups have sought to break down the barriers and make the theatre once more relevant to the masses. Many have left theatre buildings behind altogether and have moved into the streets and other public places in order to reach that audience which would not voluntarily attend the traditional theatre.

The battle lines that have been drawn are roughly comparable to those between the contemplative and the active life. Is it enough to understand, or is understanding superfluous if it does not lead to action? The question is a familiar one nowadays in universities. But it is not a new one. Similarly, there has been a continuing battle through the centuries over whether art is essentially contemplative or attuned to the world of the moment. Is it primarily idealist or realist? The idealist considers it the mission of art to show the patterns behind life and to provide man with some vision of the human condition; the realist considers it the function of art to represent life as it is observed and to provide a faithful picture of the world in which man lives. Although both may be found in almost every period, usually one dominates. Furthermore, the precise turn that each takes differs according to the assumptions of an age about man and the world he inhabits. It should be helpful, therefore, to look briefly at some manifestations of the two streams during recent centuries, for they reveal much about today's theatre.

Let us begin with the 1950s, a decade on which some now look back with nostalgia, for that was a time when the most typical student response was, "I don't want to get involved." The threat of extinction by atomic warfare hung over the period, as did the demand for ideological conformity. It was an era of anxiety. The play which best captures the spirit of that time is Beckett's *Waiting for Godot*, an outstanding example of Absurdist drama. It shows two derelicts, caught between hope and despair, who improvise diversions to pass the time while they wait for Godot to arrive. But each day ends in disappointment and they begin all over again. Numerous interpretations have been suggested for this play, but it seems most important to realize that it is about the human condition—about aspirations and hopes and the necessity of going on, even in the face of disappointment. The characters do not give in to despair, though they are often tempted to do so. Somehow they always find the courage to continue day by day.

Waiting for Godot is a detached drama, for it is more concerned with exploring man's relation to his universe than it is with suggesting any path of action. In Beckett's world, action would be useless, except to kill time. Other Absurdist dramatists were concerned with social and ideological matters, but all reached much the same conclusion that Beckett did—that this is an irrational world—

and all seemed content not to go beyond that conclusion. In fact, most seemed paralyzed by it.

Since it was Albert Camus who supplied the term by which this drama was to be known, let us look for a moment at his conception of the absurd. According to Camus, man is born with a longing for order and meaning, which he seeks to fulfill. But he soon discovers that the world is without reason. The gulf between man's hopes and desires and the irrationality of the world is the state that Camus calls absurd. As he puts it: "I said that the world is absurd, but I was too hasty. This world in itself is not reasonable, that is all that can be said. But what is absurd is the confrontation of this irrational [world] and the wild longing for clarity whose call echoes in the human heart. The absurd depends as much on man as on the world." [5] To Camus, absurdity seemed the fundamental human condition, but rather than acceding to it, he considered it a challenge. Consequently, he argued that man should deny the absurd by creating order—by choosing a position and acting consistently in accordance with it. The dramatists we call Absurdists accepted Camus's conception of an irrational universe, but rejected his challenge to defy absurdity by going beyond it.

I would like to jump back now to the Romantic era at the beginning of the nineteenth century and look at another kind of detached drama. It may appear an odd leap—from Absurdism to Romanticism—but it is not so

[5] Albert Camus, *The Myth of Sisyphus and Other Essays*, trans. Justin O'Brien (New York, 1955), 21.

strange as it may at first seem, for there are interesting parallels between the views of Camus and of Immanuel Kant, the German philosopher who set forth the ideas upon which many Romantics built.[6]

Kant, like Camus, begins by declaring that man is born with an innate desire for harmony. He describes it in different terms, for to Kant this inborn urge is a moral sense which commands men to choose virtuously. Also like Camus, Kant concludes that the world is such that man cannot satisfy this innate longing. Both, then, ascribe to man much the same basic condition. The difference comes when they seek to explain how man can overcome the barriers to fulfillment. As we have seen, Camus concluded that the universe is irrational and that man's position is absurd, unless he challenges the absurdity by creating the order that is missing in the world. Kant agrees that man's position would be absurd were there no way of fulfilling his innate desires. But in this inborn sense he sees proof that there is another realm—that of immortality—in which that sense can find full scope.

The significant difference between Kant and Camus, then, lies not so much in their conceptions of man's condition as in their conceptions of God. Had Kant not believed in God, he would have been an absurdist. Instead, through a complex series of arguments, he proves the existence of God from the innate sense he finds in man.

[6] Immanuel Kant's basic philosophical position was set forth in *The Critique of Pure Reason* (1781) and *The Critique of Practical Reason* (1788). His ideas on art are contained in *The Critique of Judgment* (1790).

On the other hand, Camus refuses to consider God or immortality as possibilities. Hence, in his world, man can only fall back on his own resources, whereas in Kant's world man's task is to reconcile his material and spiritual natures. Kant's is essentially an optimistic view, since, regardless of the shortcomings of this life, man always has the possibility of eternal bliss in an afterlife. The differences between the tone of Romantic and Absurdist drama is largely due to these differing views of man's condition.

Although not all Romantics built directly upon Kant's ideas, most of them accepted a similar view of man, whom they saw as a creature divided against himself, since his longings for perfection are constantly thwarted by the compromises he is forced to make as a participant in the material world.[7] In other words, the spirit is constantly being subverted by the flesh, or at least by the world. Since they believed that the spirit is man's most abiding element, the Romantics, not surprisingly, came to view the spiritual as more important than the material, and their drama shows how man rises above the limitations of the flesh. The hero of Romantic drama may be a misunderstood genius, a man driven by circumstances to become an outlaw, a victim of mistaken values, or a ruler who fails to achieve his goals, but the resolution of the

[7] This view underlies, for example, August Wilhelm von Schlegel's *Lectures on Dramatic Art and Literature* (1809–11), a major statement of the Romantic vision. For a full treatment, see René Wellek, *A History of Modern Criticism* (4 vols.; New Haven, Conn., 1955), II, and M. H. Abrams, *The Mirror and the Lamp: Romantic Theory and the Critical Tradition* (New York, 1953).

drama almost always establishes his worthiness by showing him choose a physical over a spiritual death. In this way, the hero affirms man's claims to the divine even in the face of destruction. During this period it was often stated that the task of art is "to make the supersensuous sensuous." [8] That is, art's ultimate concerns are with the spiritual realm, but before that realm can be apprehended it must be embodied in sensuous form if it is to communicate with finite man—the audience. Art was also considered a mediator between the physical and the spiritual worlds, for the aesthetic experience created by an artwork was said to permit man to experience momentarily freedom from the pulls of his material existence. This effect Kant described as "disinterested contemplation." A true aesthetic judgment upon an artwork, then, must be completely free from any considerations of the work's usefulness, function, or goodness. The aesthetic experience consists of "disinterested satisfaction." [9] It is probably impossible to conceive a more detached vision; nothing could be further from today's notion of the need for commitment in art.

A third conception of detached art is found near the end of the nineteenth century in the art-for-art's-sake movement. At the beginning of this section, I quoted a passage by Oscar Wilde, a leader of this school. I now repeat it, since it shows so clearly the influence of Kant:

[8] Among those who made such statements are Schiller, Coleridge, and Hegel.

[9] Immanuel Kant, *Critique of Judgment*, trans. J. H. Bernard (New York, 1951), 37–45.

"The only beautiful things are the things that do not concern us. As long as a thing is useful or necessary to us, or affects us in any way, either for pain or pleasure . . . it is outside the proper sphere of art." But the resemblance to Kant's views is superficial, for Wilde and his associates divorced their ideas from the concern with spiritual perfection which had undergirded Kant's. Instead, they looked upon art as something which gives each moment of material existence a greater intensity. As Walter Pater put it, "Art comes to you professing frankly to give nothing but the highest quality to your moments as they pass, and simply for those moments' sake." He went on to say: "A counted number of pulses only is given to us of a variegated, dramatic life. How may we see in them all that is to be seen in them by the finest senses? How shall we pass most swiftly from point to point, and be present always at the focus where the greatest number of vital forces unite in their purest energy? To burn always with this hard, gemlike flame, to maintain this ecstasy, is success in life." [10]

Here we have a totally different conception of art than that of either the Romantics or the Absurdists, who above all were concerned with the human condition. Exponents of the art-for-art's-sake outlook, on the other hand, were interested in art as a means of honing the senses so that life might be lived more intensely. Implicit in their view is the conviction that only a few can hope to achieve this

---

[10] Walter Pater, "Conclusion to *Studies in the History of the Renaissance*," in *Literary Criticism: Pope to Croce*, ed. G. W. Allen and H. H. Clark (New York, 1941), 526–30.

state, for only a few are sufficiently sensitive to appreciate the finest art. Here is the elitist conception of art in its most intense form.

Because Wilde and his associates wished to differentiate their views from those being advocated by their Realist and Naturalist contemporaries, they tended to emphasize form and technical excellence over content. Thus, Wilde says, "To art's subject matter we should be more or less indifferent." [11] The eventual results of such a view are most evident in the visual arts. In painting, recognizable subject matter has been downgraded in favor of line, color, texture, and spatial relationships, for these, instead of subject, are said to constitute the essence of painting. In the theatre, there has at times been a self-conscious use of the medium—that is, attention is called to the theatrical means themselves—but, perhaps because of its nature, the theatre has been subjected to much less abstractionism than have the visual arts. Nevertheless, the twentieth century has seen attempts in all the arts to create pure forms to be judged and valued for the way the means inherent in the medium are used rather than for any message or likeness to real life.

With the trend toward formalism came the alienation of the general public from art. Most persons still do not appreciate abstract painting, atonal music, Absurdist drama, and other artistic expressions which seem to them overly formalistic. The point is not whether they are correct, but that the very term *art* as a designation is now

[11] Wilde, "The Decay of Lying," 17.

restricted to a limited range of works which are for the most part incomprehensible to the public at large. It is also used as a value term reserved for those works which are considered sufficiently superior to others that they can be placed in this special category. The result has been to suggest that art is something which only the special few can appreciate and that the works enjoyed by the general public are inferior and debased. One often encounters today the paradoxical situation in which the public is blamed for not supporting the arts while at the same time art is defined so as to exclude the general public from whatever benefits it is supposed to confer. Yet the obvious question—why should the public support something that has nothing to do with it?—is almost never asked. It is above all this elitist view of art against which many theatre groups are now rebelling.

I have reviewed three manifestations of detached art. They differ from each other in many respects, but they share the aim of increasing perception or understanding, of being sufficiently detached or distanced from the fray to permit disinterested contemplation of human experience and through the contemplation to induce new understanding or sharpened sensitivity. They are not concerned with how the audience should apply the increased perception.

Now, let us look at some manifestations of commitment in art, which like detachment has taken varying forms in successive eras. In the modern world, Realism and Naturalism first sought to give art a practical mission. Perhaps because they were in rebellion against the

Romantic outlook, they virtually reversed the Romantic vision of man. They sought to focus attention upon the material world and, through observation, analysis, and objectivity, to help audiences better understand the causes of contemporary problems so that solutions might be found. They concluded that the theatre must become useful or perish. Alexandre Dumas *fils* said of his own work: "I realize that the prime requisites of a play are laughter, tears, passion, emotion, interest, curiosity: . . . but I maintain that if, by means of all of these ingredients . . . I can exercise some influence over society; if, instead of treating effects I can treat causes; if, for example, while I satirize and describe and dramatize adultery I can find means to force people to discuss the problem, and the law-maker to revise the law, I shall have done more than my part as a dramatist, I shall have done my duty as a man." [12]

The Naturalists were especially contemptuous of their predecessors' concern with theatrical effectiveness, which was said to distort truth. Émile Zola declares, "The word *art* displeases me; it contains I know not what ideas of necessary arrangement." [13] He wanted the writer to be rigorously, even scientifically objective so that drama might give a truthful picture of social ills and contribute to their reformation. Since in this period many of the ills were considered taboo in polite conversation or public

[12] Alexandre Dumas *fils*, "Letter to M. Sarcey," in *European Theories of the Drama*, edited by Barrett H. Clark and revised by Henry Popkin (New York, 1965), 371.
[13] Émile Zola, *Le Naturalisme au théâtre* (Paris, 1881), 16.

entertainments, it is not surprising that when the Realists and Naturalists insisted upon writing plays about
them the response was outrage. In fact, it was not new
techniques so much as new subjects that brought the
Realists their notoriety.

Ibsen's *Ghosts* became a storm center throughout
Europe, for not only did it suggest that a woman should
leave her husband if they are incompatible, it brought
the subject of venereal disease onto the stage. George Bernard Shaw took considerable delight in recalling the critical reactions to Ibsen's play when it was first performed
in England in 1891—at a private performance, it should
be noted, since the Lord Chamberlain refused to license
it for public consumption. Here are a few of the reactions to what is now considered a classic of the modern
stage: "An open drain; a loathsome sore unbandaged
... a mass of vulgarity, egotism, coarseness, and absurdity.
... A piece to bring the stage into disrepute and dis-
honour with every right-thinking man and woman. . . .
As foul and filthy a concoction as has ever been allowed
to disgrace the boards of an English theatre." [14] This
response is not unlike that to some recent productions in
New York.

Although the Realists and Naturalists were interested
in social reform, they did not, for the most part, suggest
what action should be taken. Rather, they were convinced
that it was their duty to remain as objective as possible

[14] Quoted in George Bernard Shaw, *The Quintessence of Ibsen-
ism* (New York, 1957), 91–93. This book was originally published
in 1891 and in revised form in 1913.

in their treatments of existing problems. They assumed that when the problem was clear the necessary remedies would be discovered and applied.

Let us turn now to a second type of committed art—the Epic Theatre evolved by Bertolt Brecht during the 1920s and 1930s, and which has attracted increasing notice since World War II.[15] Brecht, like the Realists and Naturalists, was concerned with reforming society, but unlike them, he was not interested in recording contemporary life faithfully. He believed, instead, that it is much more effective to use stories taken from other times or places as a basis for dramatic parables designed to comment upon contemporary society. He declared his wish that audiences watch these parables critically, judge them, and apply what they see and decide to life outside the theatre. To subvert the audience's predisposition to view a play as mere recreation, he used many devices—some of them taken over from the formalistic experiments of the art-for-art's-sake school—to keep the spectator aware that he is in the theatre watching a fictional event and that the real problems are not those in the drama but those outside the theatre. His plays are issue-centered. They seek to make the audience aware of the need for change in society and of their role in bringing about the changes. Nevertheless, Brecht maintains a neutral stance. That is, he pretends not to have any specific remedy in mind, although it is generally agreed that he

[15] Bertolt Brecht's ideas are set forth in *Brecht on Theatre*, trans. John Willett (New York, 1964), and above all in "A Short Organum for the Theatre," 179–205.

favored a socialistic or communistic society. But he avoids saying so in his plays and instead declares that the audience must make up its own mind about what should be done. Thus, at the end of one of his plays, we find this passage:

> How could a better ending be arranged?
> Could one change people? Can the world be changed?
> Would new gods do the trick? Will atheism?
> Moral rearmament? Materialism?
> It is for you to find a way, my friends,
> To help good men arrive at happy ends.
> *You* write the happy ending to the play.
> There must, there must, there's got to be a way.[16]

Thus, while Brecht thought it the purpose of drama to induce commitment and to lead to action, he avoided specifying the action to be taken.

Now, let us turn to commitment in current drama. Like Brecht and the Realists, many contemporary dramatists are interested in reshaping society, but unlike their predecessors, they do not pretend to be objective. More characteristically, they take the line adopted by Aristophanes, for they begin with a partisan position and, rather than asking that the alternatives be considered objectively, they merely seek acquiescence to the view already reached.

[16] Epilogue to *The Good Woman of Setzuan* in *Parables for the Theatre: Two Plays by Bertolt Brecht*, trans. Eric Bentley (Minneapolis, 1961) .

Let us look at an example. *Chicago 70,*[17] based on the conspiracy trial of the "Chicago Seven," is, according to publicity released by the producer, designed "to expose the sadism and brutality of the United States power structure." It is composed of actual episodes from the trial interspersed with "heavily ironic song-and-dance" sequences. Through "constant references to the trial scene in 'Alice in Wonderland'" it seeks to point up the essential madness behind the whole proceedings. "All the defendants and their lawyer are [depicted as] heroes and wits, and the judge and prosecution [as] knaves and fools." [18] What one thinks about this production depends primarily upon what one thinks about the basic premise and about the actual trial, for it is clearly not intended to offer an objective view of the proceedings. This play also relies upon many of the devices used by Aristophanes: schematized characterization, exaggerated situation, songs, dances, high spirits that range from zaniness to near-lunacy. It employs sensuous appeals of all sorts to sweep the audience along despite any desire to resist or to question.

Chicago 70 probably appeals primarily to those already in agreement with its point of view. In this fact lies another paradox of the current demand that the theatre cease to be an elitist art: many of those who seek to at-

[17] *Chicago 70* was developed and partially improvised by the Toronto Workshop Company, directed by George Luscombe. It was presented in New York in June, 1970.
[18] From a review of the production by Jack Kroll, in *Newsweek,* June 8, 1970, p. 90. Another review can be found in the New York *Times,* June 7, 1970, Section 2, p. 3.

tract the common man are the very ones who most offend him by taking up repugnant political or moral stances and by using puzzling theatrical devices. In such ways, the stated aim of ending the elitism in the theatre is often subverted.

Some groups, on the other hand, are very much attuned to the working-class audience and seek to reach it through simple, direct means. For example, El Teatro Campesino, a company based in California, addresses itself primarily to Mexican-American farm workers. In one of its plays,[19] a newly arrived Mexican is duped into taking a job not under union supervision. The Mexican works hard, but at the end of the season his money ends up in the pockets of the white landowner and when winter comes he barely avoids starvation. When the next year rolls around, the worker signs with the union and his lot is vastly improved. All this is shown in a skitlike play which uses exaggerated characters and cartoonlike situations. It is simple, direct, clearly understandable. Whether or not it is art is another question, but one that the company would consider irrelevant. No doubt it is

[19] This play was featured on the National Educational Television (NET) Playhouse's program about El Teatro Campesino, shown in May, 1970. El Teatro Campesino was founded in Delano, California, in 1965 "by Luis Valdez and members of the National Farm Workers Association to dramatize the issues of the Delano grape strike and urge farm workers to join the union. El Teatro Campesino has since become a bilingual theatre company which not only teaches and organizes Chicano workers but also enhances Mexican-Americans' pride in their cultural and ethnic heritage." Program for Radical Theatre Festival, 10.

very effective propaganda in the fight to unionize California's farm workers.

Thus, both detached art and committed art may take many forms. In both, the artist seeks to cope with fundamental truths, to reflect reality as he sees it. But the detached artist tends to view it as his mission to increase understanding and perception, whereas the committed artist sees it as his role to provide a basis for action. Our judgment about which is detached and which committed depends in part upon our psychological relationship to the works—upon what is sometimes called "aesthetic distance," or the degree to which we are able to contemplate an artwork dispassionately. The more personal a play becomes, the greater our involvement; when our values are threatened, we become less dispassionate, less uncommitted in our responses. Thus, even committed art varies widely in its capacity to affect us. Plays that to nineteenth-century audiences seemed "committed" may now impress us as "detached" because they no longer have any direct effect on our lives. On the other hand, we often feel deeply about such plays as *Chicago 70* because it is impossible to remain detached when our values and convictions are being attacked or sustained.

No doubt many of us would prefer to go back a few years to a time when a visit to the theatre was not so apt to be an unsettling occasion. One can, of course, still find plays that are intended primarily to enlighten or divert, but the proportion of noncommitted drama appears to lessen yearly. In this, however, the theatre is merely a reflection of its society, which also has become increasingly divided into camps, each making exclusive claims to our allegiance. When society is healed, no doubt the theatre will become less militant and art more detached.

SIX / Redefining Theatre

Behind all the topics I have discussed—changing values, structural patterns, intellectual and emotional appeals, detachment and commitment—lurks another: the desire to redefine theatre. In fact, all these issues represent attempts to alter traditional patterns, to open up new possibilities, to make the theatre more responsive to the needs of the age. Consequently, in this concluding section, I shall explore some directions of change and their implications.

Current innovations can be seen in clearer perspective by setting them in the context of earlier attitudes about the theatre and its role in society. If we go back to the beginning of recorded history—that is, before there was a theatre in our sense—we find all the theatrical elements already in use, but as a part of religious ritual rather than as an autonomous activity. The steps whereby drama was separated from ritual are unclear, but they were taken by the Greeks during the sixth century B.C. Despite our lack of specific information about these early developments, it seems reasonably certain that theatre evolved out of sacred rites. For many centuries it retained a semi-religious function, since until the Renaissance performances were normally associated with religious festivals. Furthermore, until the end of the Middle Ages, it was supported financially by the government or church; it was not a commercial venture. It was also for the most part occasional—that is, plays were presented only at festivals or at similar special events rather than continuously throughout the year.

Then, at the end of the medieval period, the church gradually withdrew its sanction and support; at the same time, because of the close connections between church and state, civil authorities withdrew their financial support, although they grudgingly permitted actors to perform for paying audiences. Thus, acting troupes now had to depend on entrance fees. At this time, dramatists were also forbidden to treat religious subjects. Therefore, the theatre became both secular and commercial. As a consequence, the nature of the theatre changed during the Renaissance, for there is a significant difference between a business venture and a celebration offered in the name of the community and church. The change has influenced all subsequent developments.[1]

So long as the theatre was essentially ceremonial and occasional and so long as it was open to everyone without charge, the primary need in theatre architecture was to provide adequately for seeing and hearing and for accommodating large numbers of persons, but when the

[1] For an overview of these developments, see Oscar G. Brockett, *History of the Theatre* (Boston, 1968), and Richard Southern, *The Seven Ages of the Theatre* (New York, 1961).

theatre became a commercial venture, other considerations began to dominate. If performances were to yield revenue, access to them had to be controlled so that fees might be collected from all those who entered and so those who did not pay could not see or hear. (Although one may merely take up a collection at an out-of-door assembly, this is not a very satisfactory guarantee of income, since whether or how much each spectator gives cannot be controlled.) Additionally, there was a need to protect both audiences and performers against inclement weather, for a commercial venture is risky if it can be interrupted at any time by unpredictable conditions. Consequently, the theatre moved indoors after centuries of outdoor playing.

The buildings that evolved during the seventeenth century were also influenced by the class structure of society. If patrons were to attend the theatre enthusiastically and often, they had to be provided certain guarantees against association with undesirable persons. The result was an auditorium divided into boxes, pit (or what is now called the orchestra), and gallery (or top balcony). The affluent and "respectable" patrons tended to sit in boxes, which were small, relatively costly, and private. In the gallery, sight lines were so bad and the seats so cheap that it became the haunt of the poor. The pit was most often occupied by men about town; occasionally women sat there, although in some countries they were forbidden to do so.

This attempt to woo all classes was reflected as well in the evening's bill, which became increasingly complex, especially after industrialization and urbanization swelled the ranks of potential patrons among the lower and middle classes. Not only was the bill changed nightly, but each program sought through some element to please each taste. A play by Shakespeare might be followed by a farce or musical drama, and between the acts variety entertainment of all kinds was given: singing, dancing, comic routines, trained animals, acrobats, and so on. Established stars were mingled with novelties of various sorts in an attempt to attract the widest possible audience. Often an evening's program lasted for five hours or more.

But, in the last half of the nineteenth century, all this gradually changed. As the size of the potential audience increased, it became apparent to some managers that they need not appeal to all segments of the public but could survive on the patronage of one part. Consequently, they began to offer programs much more restricted in scope and range of appeal. Variety acts were excluded from dramatic programs and were performed in their own special theatres (in England music halls flourished, as did vaudeville in America). As the evening's bill was sorted out, so was the audience, as various segments went to theatres catering to their particular tastes. The overall consequence was to make each theatre's audience relatively homogeneous. As this occurred, the need for a segregated auditorium also vanished; boxes were abandoned, and the orchestra, the most advantageous location for seeing and hearing, became the place most favored by patrons.

Thus, by the end of the nineteenth century, the theatre had become fragmented, for the various types of entertainment had been separated from each other and their differing appeals had led to a corresponding division in the audience. Now there began a process in which each of these parts was decimated by competition from other types of entertainment. Spectator sports and motion pictures eventually attracted most of the lower-class patrons; the upper classes had long favored opera and other similar activities. The process was complex, but by the 1930s, and perhaps earlier, audiences for dramatic entertainment—that is, for the live performance of plays —were being drawn primarily from the middle class.

With this narrowing of the audience went a narrowing of taste. The middle class has never been noted for its adventurousness, and in appealing to it managers in the commercial theatre have tended to follow the path of conservatism both in programming and in production. As Eric Bentley has observed, the whole weight of the theatre "goes into the effort to repeat former successes rather than create new ones. To duplicate, not to originate, is the aim and the method. Hence, if Broadway people take up a work that is different, they change it till it is the same. The Broadway critics have no higher praise for a classic than to say that it is as good as the latest commercial hit; and the Broadway producer's way with a classic is to make sure that it is identical with the latest commercial hit." [2] Although perhaps extreme, this view is certainly grounded in truth.

[2] Eric Bentley, *What Is Theatre? Incorporating the Dramatic Event and Other Reviews, 1944–1967* (New York, 1968), vii.

As Bentley suggests, commercial managers have also tended to favor some version of realistic presentation—that is, the easily understood, relatively lifelike (or at least familiar) approach in both story and production style. This is another heritage from the past, for, since the Renaissance, the theatre has been devoted to illusionism. In fact, the picture-frame stage was invented to enhance the seeming reality of painted settings. The fiction that one is watching real people in real situations and in real places is the essence of the proscenium stage. That the picture-frame theatre remains dominant indicates the power that illusionism still exerts over audiences, even though today's illusionism differs considerably from that of a century ago.

It should be clear from this brief survey that many forces—some social and economic, others artistic—have helped to shape the theatre of our time. I have argued that the Broadway theatre has for the most part become the preserve of the affluent middle class, that its major productional style is a modified (or simplified) realism, and that the range of its offerings, means, and appeals is severely limited. It is these established patterns that many contemporary practitioners wish to modify. Some reformers are concerned with turning the theatre away from its commercial outlook and back toward the position it originally occupied as a meaningful expression of all the people. Most have more limited goals. Not all of these can be treated here, but their major thrust can be suggested by looking briefly at those areas in which changes are underway.

Some of the most obvious and least controversial reforms involve theatre architecture. The agitation for change in this area began slowly in the late nineteenth century when a few directors came to realize that Greek and Shakespearean plays might fare better in an arrangement more nearly like those in use when they were written than the picture-frame stage could provide. Max Reinhardt was especially instrumental in the movement toward seeking the most effective spatial arrangement for each play. But his were only some among many experiments with staging Greek dramas in circuses, Shakespearean plays on open platforms, and works from other periods in still other ways.

Despite these occasional attempts, there was no really strong impetus toward architectural change until after World War II. Since that time there has been much concern for flexible theatres which permit the rearrangement of the elements to create a variety of spatial relationships. But most of these flexible theatres have been judged unsatisfactory, since they seem to demand too many compromises in each arrangement in order to include several possibilities in a single structure. Consequently, most recent buildings seek flexibility by including more than one theatre in the same structure rather than by seeking to make the same theatre alterable. The proscenium-arch theatre seems still to be the favorite, but there has been a marked movement toward two other basic types: the arena stage (with the audience surrounding the acting area on all sides) and the thrust stage (with the audience seated around three sides of a raised platform, often backed by a modified proscenium stage).

This concern for new spatial arrangements is one of the most characteristic features of the contemporary theatre, even among otherwise conservative groups. It is symptomatic of our redefinition of illusionism, for we no longer demand full representation but are now willing to accept fragmentary and suggestive scenery. Nevertheless, it would be a mistake to assume that most groups are no longer concerned with representationalism, for, even on arena and thrust stages, most still emphasize psychologically realistic performance and use characteristic setpieces or properties to suggest place.

Many practitioners today, however, consider any fixed arrangement of seats and stage too confining and prefer merely a large room—an open space. The off-Broadway and off-off-Broadway theatres have exploited this approach most fully. For example, in New York the Performance Group operates in an old garage, while others use lofts, warehouses, churches, and similar buildings. Such open space permits maximum flexibility in manipulating and adjusting the relationship between the audience and the performers. Jerzy Grotowski, director of the Polish Laboratory Theatre, has perhaps exploited the open space most fully.[3] He insists that each production must be designed in its totality—including the audience—and that the ideal number and ideal placement of the spectators vary with each play. Consequently, in his productions the space given over to the audience—the number of seats and their arrangement—is designed as care-

[3] Grotowski's work is described most fully in Jerzy Grotowski, *Towards a Poor Theatre* (New York, 1968).

fully as is that used by the actors. When the Polish Laboratory Theatre performed in New York in 1970 it created considerable controversy for many reasons but not the least because of Grotowski's adamant insistence that the audience be limited, not in accordance with the theatre's capacity but to fit each production's demands. The performances were shifted from a theatre to a church and the seating rearranged for each play according to Grotowski's specifications.[4] Such a demand seemed novel indeed in New York, where the aim is to attract the largest possible number of spectators (including standees, when fire regulations permit). Even the off-off-Broadway producers, who frequently scorn Broadway, discovered that they had not escaped commercialism as much as they had imagined.

But to many contemporary theatre workers, any building, whether a traditional theatre or a warehouse, seems too inhibiting, for they see in the tendency to view the theatre as a place rather than as an activity one of the principal reasons for its failures. They blame much of the elitist atmosphere of the theatre on certain patterns that have become so ritualized—the whole routine of obtaining tickets, of ushers, ticket-takers, cloakroom attendants, notions of appropriate dress and behavior, and so on—and so intimidating to the uninitiated that they consider the theatre foreign to their way of life. Some would-

---

[4] Accounts of the appearances in New York can be found in the New York *Times*, October 18, 1969, p. 36; October 26, Section 2, p. 1; November 5, p. 40; November 11, p. 43; November 20, p. 60; and November 30, Section 2, pp. 1, 18.

be reformers refer to this as institutionalized theatre, and they liken it to the museum where the dead past is venerated more than the living present. To them, the theatre cannot be reformed until it is removed from this debilitating atmosphere. As they see it, the traditional theatre is devoted primarily to entertaining audiences without offending them and to discouraging those not attuned to its rituals. At the same time, they believe that the vitality of the theatre depends upon attracting a wider, less homogeneous audience.

Despairing of wooing this new spectator into existing theatres, they have sought instead to take the theatre to the people—by performing in parks, in the street, in subways, in bars, and at other places where people who do not ordinarily go to the theatre gather.[5] They try to create productions fitted to particular environments— plays that will work especially well in a playground, for example—and perform in "found space" rather than in theatre buildings. In this way, they hope to break down negative feelings about the theatre and to show ordinary people that the theatre does have something to say to them. Eventually their hope is to diversify the theatre by enlarging the audience to include a greater range of expectations and needs.

Involved in practically all the movements toward reform is the question of repertory—what kind of productions should audiences be offered? Almost everyone seems

[5] Joe Papp has especially championed these ideas, but like most others, he has talked about it more than he has actually practiced it.

to agree that the theatre should be entertaining, in the sense of catching and holding attention or engaging interest. Most of the reformers, however, demand that additionally the theatre should be made more relevant to our lives than it has been in the past. Unfortunately, relevance may be defined in various ways. Broadway producers certainly do not consider their offerings irrelevant. Rather, they offer plays so attuned to current standards that they seem neither old-fashioned nor overly strange. Popular theatre has always depended upon manipulating views acceptable to its audience. Thus, Broadway productions may not always be thoughtful, challenging, or penetrating, but they usually mirror well the popular attitudes of the day. In addition to diversionary entertainment, Broadway also supplies a sampling of thoughtful plays about the effects of social, psychological, or economic pressures on individuals—the kind of drama written by Arthur Miller, Tennessee Williams, and Edward Albee. Such works are relevant because they comment on the current scene by showing the impact of contemporary life on interesting and complex characters. But, though they imply much, they usually treat society at large only obliquely.

A third way of seeking relevance is through the production of classics in a manner to suggest some relationship between works of the past and contemporary dilemmas. For example, in 1969 the American Shakespeare Festival Company produced *Henry V* in a way calculated to make war and chauvinism seem ridiculous, especially in the

battles fought by soldiers on stilts.[6] It would be difficult
to catalogue all the productions of classics in recent years
designed, according to their directors, to show the world's
hypocrisy and depravity or man's isolation from his fellow creatures. The majority, nevertheless, retain the original texts with few major changes.

Other groups, however, have utilized the classics merely as a basis for almost wholly new creations. A good example is *Dionysus in 69*, an improvisation on Euripides'
play *The Bacchae,* presented by Richard Schechner and
his Performance Group.[7] Few of Euripides' original lines
were heard by the audience (although they may have
been spoken), for the overall impression was of multiple
actions (some of them invisible to many spectators) occurring in various parts of the theatre. Effects were gained
not through traditional means but through an accumula-
tion of vocal sound (grunts, cries, moans, whispers) and
mass action, varying from the quiet to the frenetic, from
the ecstatic to the orgiastic, culminating in simulated
ritualistic murder. Schechner seems to have had the theories of Artaud and Grotowski in mind, as well as those
of Timothy Leary about mind-expanding drugs. Thus,
Schechner intermingled many present-day interests with
the original classical text to create a wholly new work.

Somewhat similarly, Schechner later did a version of

[6] For reviews of the production, see the New York *Times,* June
9, 1969, p. 57; June 15, Section 2, p. 3; and November 11, p. 43.
[7] For a review of the production, see the New York *Times,* June
7, 1968, p. 35. The text, with many pictures, has since been published: Richard Schechner, *Dionysus in 69* (New York, 1970).

Macbeth (which he called *Makbeth*),[8] in which all the actors were dressed in gym suits and moved constantly as if on a race track. To enter the theatre, one had to pass through a maze composed largely of mirrors which forced the spectator to come face to face with himself, while on the mirror above his head certain of Macbeth's key speeches were printed so that when the spectator looked at himself he also had to read the speeches. In this and other ways, the point was made that in the race of life we tend to tread others underfoot in order to get ahead. Although we may not resort to murder, as does Macbeth, we tend nevertheless to be consumed by ambition, as he is. Thus, we are supposed to see that we too are Macbeth.

But the groups most self-conscious about relevance are those concerned with the immediate scene. They also have attracted the most attention because they have seemed most shocking and militant. Their interests vary widely. *Chicago 70,* for example, seeks to treat the immediate social, political, and ideological scene as reflected in the trial upon which it is based. *Hair* is concerned above all with justifying and advocating a new life style. *Oh! Calcutta!* seems merely interested in exploiting the current atmosphere of permissiveness by offering rather sophisticated pornography. The list could be extended endlessly, for nearly all current preoccupations have been the subject of theatrical offerings.

[8] For reviews of *Makbeth*, see the New York *Times*, October 19, 1969, Section 2, p. 27; November 21, p. 51; and November 30, Section 2, p. 3.

Some productions seem merely calculated to shock the bourgeoisie, but others sincerely seek to make the public think about values and issues and reexamine convictions and prejudices. The most militant of the groups has been the Living Theatre—at least it was the pioneering and best known of troupes. Like most radical groups of the 1950s, the Living Theatre, when it began, was interested primarily in new theatrical methods.[9] Its early productions were of plays by Gertrude Stein, William Carlos Williams, August Strindberg, Luigi Pirandello, and Jean Cocteau. Not until it had been in existence for about ten years did it become concerned with immediate relevance. After 1959, when it presented Jack Gelber's *The Connection*, it turned increasingly toward political agitation, as if believing that any theatrical reform had to await political change. Thereafter its productions were ever more militant, *Paradise Now*, its final creation, being little more than a collection of political slogans and incitements to anarchical acts. The performers invaded the auditorium, sought confrontations with the spectators, and heaped obscenities or spat on those who opposed them.[10]

Such intimidating behavior is now lessening, for the companies are becoming more sophisticated and they

[9] A history of the Living Theatre until it went into exile can be found in Charles L. Mee, Jr., "The Becks' Living Theatre," *Tulane Drama Review*, VII (1962), 194–205.

[10] About performances of this work, see the New York *Times*, September 28, 1968, p. 6, and October 15, 1968, p. 39. Interesting sidelights are offered in "Booking the Revolution," *Drama Review*, XIII (Summer, 1969), 80–88.

recognize that unless presented skillfully, political content is ineffective. R. G. Davis of the San Francisco Mime Theatre has said that his group had to choose between going to demonstrations and doing productions of high quality: "In terms of political activity, demonstrations and protests, for me, are ended. I've always said to myself that if the protest is more important than what we do in the theatre, then we should go to the protest. That means we must do something very significant. . . . People who are radical and who do not necessarily want to commit themselves to acting or the theatre for a long time, should [join guerrilla theatre troupes]. . . . But discipline, the efficiency and administration and all that stuff is absolutely necessary to achieve anything [in the theatre]." [11] About radical theatre groups, Davis says: "We are all in one way or another opposed to the plastic world of the United States, the whole middle class monstrosity. . . . success is when we do something right and other people act. . . . Success is not a good review, but creating other alternatives." [12]

Just as the desire to be relevant has led to many different kinds of plays and approaches, so too it has motivated changes in the elements of production. For example, there is now a trend toward honoring the work of the company as a unit instead of merely emphasizing that of virtuoso artists, a considerable departure from the typical practices of Broadway, which has always ex-

[11] Program for Radical Theatre Festival, San Francisco State College, September, 1968, p. 34.
[12] *Ibid.*, 12, 36.

ploited the appeal of well-known actors, writers, and directors and where scripts have often been tailored to fit the talents of starring performers. The Open Theatre has presented a number of productions which came into being through the cooperative efforts of a playwright, a director, and a group of actors.[13] The playwright supplies an outline of ideas and scenes; then the actors improvise on these situations and the script gradually takes shape as the playwright and director choose those elements which seem most effective. The production is then perfected, although portions are always improvised during performances. Plays worked out in this way include Jean-Claude van Itallie's *The Serpent* and Megan Terry's *Viet Rock*. This approach is becoming increasingly popular among college students as well.

Concern for the group as a unit is reflected in many ways. Often the programs merely list the actors' names alphabetically and do not even indicate who plays which roles. This is especially apt to be done when the same actors play many different roles. The result is to focus attention on ensemble effort rather than the work of a few.

Such groups also tend to deemphasize costume and scenery. Frequently the actors wear coveralls, leotards, or some nondescript or neutral rehearsal clothing, even though the action may be set in widely varying places

[13] For a description of the work of the Open Theatre, see Joseph Chaikin, "The Open Theatre," *Tulane Drama Review*, IX (1964), 191–97. See also the Preface to Jean-Claude van Itallie, *The Serpent: A Ceremony* (New York, 1969).

and times and even though the same actor may play a number of different roles. Changes in place are usually established through pantomime, dialogue, or the manipulation of a few set-pieces which remain onstage throughout the performance.

Many of these practices owe much to Grotowski, who through the performances of his Polish Laboratory Theatre and his writings has proclaimed the superiority of a "poor theatre"—that is, one that does not have elaborate machinery, scenery, costumes, or lighting.[14] Thus, unable to rely on the work of designers and technicians, the actor must depend entirely on his own resources. Grotowski's actors wear no makeup nor are they permitted to change costumes, although they may improvise with what they wear to create new effects. Morever, since Grotowski's company is fixed in number, the same actors play all the roles, no matter how many there are in a production. Consequently, individual performers must shift identities without the aid of costume or makeup. Similarly, no scene changes are permitted beyond what can be improvised with the properties onstage when the performance begins. Grotowski argues that the actor must master his resources so completely that out of them he can create whatever the dramatic situation requires and without appreciable external aids.

Grotowski's downgrading of scenery, costumes, and lighting is attractive to some groups because it lessens the financial burden of production. But it also accords with

14 See Grotowski, *Towards a Poor Theatre*, 15–25.

the trend away from illusionism and toward asking the audience to enter imaginatively into the performance by envisioning changes in roles, time, and place from a few clues supplied by the actors. At the same time, it emphasizes communal over individual effort. As one director has put it, "We have no stars, only a great deal of anonymity." [15]

In recent years there has also been a trend away from traditional concepts of acting. Perhaps because, since the Renaissance, the theatre has been devoted to illusionism, acting has been viewed as the art of impersonation—the ability to take on another identity. In recent years, however, it has been suggested that acting might more properly be considered *task-* rather than *personality*-oriented (that is, more concerned with the thing done than with who does it). Such a view owes much to Happenings.[16] Here the participants do not assume another identity but carry out assigned or improvised tasks; the Happening ends when all the tasks have been completed. Certainly not all Happenings (and perhaps none) are wholly dramatic, however, and consequently they do not provide as great a challenge to performers as do written texts. Moreover, practically all dramatists of the past appear to assume that performers will impersonate the characters they create. On the other hand, many recent writers have deemphasized the roles of individuals in favor of groups, the members of which are scarcely differentiated. Often

[15] R. G. Davis, in Program for Radical Theatre Festival, 36.
[16] For a discussion of the performer's function in Happenings, see Michael Kirby (ed.), *Happenings* (New York, 1966), 14–20.

the actor need not impersonate another but may remain himself, merely doing what is required. For example, in one part of *The Serpent* the performers are directed to address the audience and give their own real names, the city from which they come, and other personal information. Thus, at times they are themselves; at others they take on the identities of characters, but they do not pretend to be those characters so much as they seek to present them without denying their own selves.[17] One may argue that the difference between this and the traditional approach is merely one of degree, but it departs markedly from the Stanislavsky method, which has long been favored in America, and it clearly emphasizes actions and issues more than it does the creation of well-rounded personalities, which is the heart of Stanislavsky's approach. Consequently, the demands made on the actor differ considerably from those of the past.

Attempts to focus attention upon an ensemble and especially upon the actor and his resources are by no means universal. There has been as well another, almost contradictory effort to elevate technological means to a position of primacy. Almost everywhere scenery in the traditional sense has been downgraded in favor of electronically created scenic environments (that is, effects gained through light and sound). The new emphasis is seen at its most intense in multimedia productions in which projected still or motion pictures, stereophonic sound of

[17] These notions show the influence of Brecht, although there are key differences.

various kinds, and live actors mingle.[18] Such productions usually require multiple screens, on each of which a different image may be projected and changed often. Films may alternate with or accompany the performances of onstage actors, or closed-circuit television may show the action then in progress from many angles, provide close-ups of actors, or even show the audience itself. Stereophonic sound—ranging through music, nonverbal noises, and atmospheric effects, and varying widely in direction and volume—adds to the sensory appeals.

Multimedia productions usually embody in a rather extreme way another departure from tradition—away from the single to multiple focal points—one which can be seen as well in the productions of such companies as the Open Theatre and the Performance Group. In the past, plays have been staged so as to insure that each moment will have a single primary focus, to which the audience's attention is directed through composition and other devices. It has been assumed that everything in each scene should be visible and audible to every member of the audience. On the other hand, recent productions—and especially those done in multimedia—have challenged these assumptions by providing many competing attractions. In other kinds of productions as well, scenes have been staged so that only a part of the audience can

[18] The Czech designer Josef Svoboda has done most to perfect multimedia production. His work is discussed in Jarka Burian, "Josef Svoboda: Theatre Artist in an Age of Science," *Educational Theatre Journal*, XXII (1970), 123–45.

see them, and in some instances actors have whispered their speeches to a single spectator. Various scenes may be going on in widely separated parts of the theatre simultaneously.[19] The audience is provided with a multitude of stimuli among which it may choose.

These innovations suggest that conceptions about the human capacity to absorb sensations are changing. Just as dramatic structure is departing from the orderly sequence of cause-to-effect, so too sensuous appeals are now being offered simultaneously rather than sequentially. Those who use them assume that the spectator will take in many things directly and others peripherally and that the combination will be more complex and revealing (and more like the bombardment to which he is subjected daily) than would be the traditional focus upon a series of sequential stimuli. Involved as well is the general trend toward downgrading the spoken word in favor of communication through other means—especially sight and sound as they affect the muscles and nerves and the perception of mood and rhythm.

Other trends might be mentioned, but these are sufficient to suggest the direction of current redefinitions. Many persons attuned to the traditional theatre are inclined to question the effectiveness of the innovations and to dismiss them as misguided. No doubt many of them are. But effectiveness can be determined only after

[19] Multiple focus and simultaneous scenes are not new. They were championed by the Futurists and Dadaists in the decade between 1910 and 1920. They then fell out of favor and were reactivated by Happenings in the 1950s, and since then they have been exploited increasingly.

a fair trial. Those that are truly ineffective will be abandoned quickly enough, while those that are productive deserve acceptance. Considerable tolerance for the new seems essential, even when it means permitting some questionable practices, for a completely static theatre is not a healthy one and change is inevitable if the theatre is to survive. We may not like the direction of change, but change will come. If we take the position that only the kind of theatre we prefer should be permitted, we may find our brand outlawed if our opponents become more powerful than we are. There is no reason why we cannot and should not have several kinds of theatre side by side. In diversity is greater health than in narrow exclusiveness.

Although the attempts to redefine theatre may on the surface seem to threaten tradition, they might more correctly be seen as broadening and extending it. Today's extremes are apt to fall into disfavor under their own weight without either our help or hindrance, just as worthy elements in the past tradition will survive. Unless our age differs markedly from all previous times, the new trends will alter the received mode somewhat but will lead to a synthesis of the old and the new. The ultimate direction taken will be determined in large part by the direction taken by society itself, for the theatre must reflect those it serves.

INDEX